BALANCING LIFE WITH SMALL GAINS

Establishing yourself and finding financial freedom

BRANDON KNAPP

For everyone who has struggled, is struggling, or will struggle under poor conditions, there is a light at the end of the tunnel and your dreams can become reality, if and when you reach for them.

Balancing Life with Small Gains
Establishing yourself and finding financial freedom

Preface

The basis of this work stemmed from my continued passion and interest in the topic of *success* and how it is defined by different people, from different backgrounds. This book explores a variety of themes related to building financial stability and tries to understand the best approach. I have included personal experiences to validate some of my points that I have not revealed to many, because I do believe the lessons are invaluable for those who have not been well-educated on such matters like money management. I also explore decision-making and provide real examples of how we can heavily rely on other's successes and failures to help us make better decisions, and not necessarily need to experience the same hardships, others have experienced. The goal is to provide a perspective that may be unique, yet helpful, and if my words can inspire, then I may consider this work a success.

Acknowledgements

I could not have achieved my current level of success without a strong support group. First of all, there is my wife who has supported me with love and understanding. Secondly, God who has always been there for me, even when I am not worthy of his love. Thank you to my parents who have been long-time supporters of mine, especially when I was not doing as well and had some struggles. My brother also has supported me and continues to make me laugh. There is also my favorite Uncle Chris and grandpa 'Papi' who must also be thanked for their support and the knowledge I've gained from them. My grandparents who are not alive today including my father's mother and father, and mother's mother. These are also solid pillars in my life who in some shape or form, shaped my life by giving my mother and father incredible values that they could pass down. I can only hope they are looking down from heaven, proud of my brother and me.

And, now for the stars of the show, who have really driven me to write and finish this book. These are the people who will shape our future and I am confident they will do an amazing job at that. These are incredible kids, quickly growing up, which both saddens and excites me. I am talking about my two sons Ben and Matt, and my incredible nephew Johnny. These are the real stars who deserve all the thanks in the world for making everyone smile and realize why we are doing what we are doing. I am very proud of these three kids and dedicate this book to them.

Table of Contents

Preface..*4*

Acknowledgements...*5*

Table of Contents *6*

Chapter 1 - Introduction *9*

Chapter 2 – Commitment *32*

Chapter 3 – Learning from others *55*

Chapter 4 – Setting and tracking your goals *74*

Chapter 5 – Small Gains...*91*

Chapter 6 – My family *107*

Chapter 7 - Retirement *123*

Chapter 8 – Financial Stability *140*

Chapter 9 – Building your career *155*

Chapter 10 – Opportunities for success.................*173*

Chapter 11 – Lifestyle for success........................*188*

Chapter 12 – Perseverance *196*

Chapter 13 – Balancing Life with Small Gains *207*

"I never attempt to make money on the stock market. I buy on the assumption that they could close the market the next day and not reopen it for ten years."

– Warren Buffett

Chapter 1 - Introduction

50 miles east of Detroit, you will find a small city called Chatham in the Province of Ontario, Canada. At one time Chatham had three large manufacturing plants that provided jobs to thousands of local residents. Libby's famous for their canned meat and vegetable products. Campbell Soup Company famous for their soup. Navistar famous for their truck manufacturing. Additionally, there was a large Heinz plant nearby in Leamington, which is 35 miles away. Business around these parts were booming, or at least that is what I was told.

The Chatham Libby's plant closed down in 1985. The Chatham Campbell's plant closed down in 1993. The Chatham Navistar plant closed down in 2011. The Leamington Heinz plant closed down in 2014. So as they say, nothing good lasts forever.

After these manufacturers closed up, a good portion of the good paying jobs in Chatham went away. Thousands of people were left without jobs. It's a 1-hour drive northeast to London or west to Windsor, to larger cities with more career opportunities. There is also the option of moving northeast to Toronto, which is 3-hours away. For many of these factory workers who lost their jobs, moving to another town could be a very big challenge. Many of these people lived in Chatham their entire lives and worked for more than 30-years in these factories. Additionally, it was rare to have the company ask you to relocate. There were only a handful of people at each of these companies given the opportunity to relocate, after they shut the factory doors.

In 1993 when Campbell's plant closed in Chatham, my father was one of the lucky ones who was offered the opportunity to relocate with the company. He was given the option of relocating to Toronto or Campbell's World Headquarters in Camden, New Jersey. Based on the high cost of living in Toronto, my father and mother decided Camden would better suit our family. At the time I was 8-years old and my brother was 11-years old. It was not the ideal situation, but jobs were extremely limited in Chatham. My father was in his early thirties and had already been 8-years with Campbell's. Relocating to their headquarters was very promising for his career. It was also a ticket into the United States with all expenses paid by someone else.

After moving to New Jersey, we would visit Chatham frequently because all of our family still lived there. Thanksgiving, Christmas, Easter, spring break, and summers we were visiting. For many years, my brother and I spent our summers in Chatham with our Uncle and Grandpa. New Jersey was different and I always wanted to move back because I missed our relatives in Chatham. Specifically, our cousins who we were very close with. Back then, I was a little bitter about the move, but knew it was right for our family. The summers spent in Chatham with my family were extremely helpful. My uncle would teach me so much, especially about being smart with money.

My uncle worked for Navistar for many years and was very mindful of how he spent his money. Many of his co-workers bought large houses, boats, and expensive cars because they were making great money working for Navistar. Employees sweeping the factory were making over $20 per hour. For a small town and a low responsibility job, that was great money. My uncle was much smarter than that! He saved his money and worked on paying off his mortgage before purchasing frivolous things. When Navistar closed, my uncle was one of the few that was still able to live a nice life and didn't lose everything he bought.

We all live our lives the best way we know how and there is nothing wrong with that. Some people are making millions of dollars each year doing what they love. Others are living below the poverty line not doing what they love. There's also the in between. We want to be respected by others and feel important. We want to earn as much money as possible. We want to take luxurious vacations and have our friends envy us. We want to live the best lives we can.

Yesterday, I went to Washington DC for the day to tour the city and watch a baseball game. This is a city where some of the most powerful people in the world work. The news provides us with updates about current events and stories happening in Washington. A lot of these stories do not feel real when I watch them on TV. When I visit Washington DC, I quickly realize it's real. There's a lot of power in Washington. The buildings are incredibly large and robust. There's a great number of people walking around wearing expensive suits, with their badges hanging from lanyards around their necks. These are the people making big decisions for America.

I think about myself and ask, *how do I compare to Washington and the people here?* We are all different, yet we all want to be somewhat the same. We want to be successful with power, respect, and wealth. We don't want to feel insignificant. I have judged others based on what they were wearing, what they were driving, and who they were with. If someone is poorly dressed, driving a junky car, and hanging around with poor people, I'd assume they are probably not very successful. Although this is most likely true, it is not always true. Some of the wealthiest people I know do not dress in a suit every day or drive a luxury car. They may not feel the need to prove themselves to others because they know inside, they already made it.

Success has been a topic of interest for me starting in high school about my sophomore or junior year. I knew stocking shelves at a local supermarket for $6/hour would not allow me to live the life I wanted to live. During this time in my life, I did not know exactly what I wanted to do, but I knew I wanted to be successful. Defining success was a challenge in itself. I quickly realized success is not defined exactly the same for everyone. During my years in high school, I've changed my mind on what I thought I wanted to do countless times. Even in college, I changed my mind on what I wanted to do countless times. After college, I also changed direction several times.

In my life, I've met all types of people from all walks of life. You can have two people in the same role that got there in two very different ways. Some people know exactly what they want to do from day one. Others, similar to me do not know exactly what they want to do and discover their passions along the way. Either way is fine, as long as you put some guidelines in place to start. As we all know, setting goals is a must. In this book, I am going to take you through various success topics based on personal experiences and learnings.

Surfing the internet on Saturday, March 23, 2019, I found an article at www.makingsenseofcents.com titled – *10 Statistics About The Money Habits of The Average American*. According to this article, *the average American household has **$132,529 worth of debt***. According to an article on CNBC.com titled, *US median household income climbs to new high of $61,372*, the **median household income was $61,372** in 2017.

Based on the median household ***income of $61,372***, we could assume ***$132,529 worth of debt*** could be removed in two to three years. This is a false assumption because we do not actually take home the full $61,372 each year due to expenditures. We can expect to pay roughly $12,000 in tax on $60,000 each year. This includes Federal and State income tax, social security, and Medicare tax. We would also expect to contribute funds for medical insurance, auto insurance, home insurance, utilities, and food to just name a few. These costs are dependent on your living situation. Better insurance obviously cost more. Insuring higher priced items will obviously cost more. Utilities for a larger house will cost more. Higher quality foods will cost more. These types of expenditures do not contribute to the removal of your debt.

The $132,529 worth of debt is the amalgamation of your mortgage, auto loan, and credit card debt. Each of these debts held by a lender will charge you interest. We can use 5% annual percentage rate (APR) in this example. This means, for every $100,000 you owe, you are paying $5,000 per year in interest. Since you are allocating the bulk of your annual income to normal living expenses and very little to debt, you are slowly paying off your debt. Remember your normal living expenses include auto insurance, home insurance, utilities, food, and any other regularly occurring expenditure, not including loans. Imagine you only pay $10,000 worth of debt each year. This means in three years you are just getting the $132K down to $100K. If you are paying $5,000 in interest per year based on the 5% APR for three years, then you've paid $15,000 in interest in just three years. You still owe $100K and will end up paying a lot more interest by the time you completely paid the loan off.

For most people, this becomes a conundrum because they feel they have no choice, but to live paycheck to paycheck. In our example, we are paying $15,000 in interest in just three years. In just three short years, we gave away $15,000 that could have been used for greater things. Lenders are lending their money to borrowers to earn money. Lenders are normally banks, credit unions, mortgage brokers, and sometimes the government. A good example of a type of loan the government may provide is a federal student loan. Loans are not necessarily a bad thing, but we need to keep an open mind and shop around if we do need one. Not all banks are going to give you the same mortgage rates and terms. Remember, banks are looking to make money and grow their business. As they say, nothing is free.

Another statistic from the article, *10 Statistics About the Money Habits of The Average American* is, *30% of American households have a long-term financial plan.* This implies 70% of Americans do not have a long-term financial plan. This is quite concerning for a variety of reasons. Can you imagine jumping on an airplane and flying to Tokyo, Japan with no return ticket? Not only do you not have a return ticket, but you also don't have hotel reservations, luggage, and don't know the language. You are flying thousands of miles away for an unspecified time with no plan. As crazy as that is, I think it is crazier to go through life without a long-term financial plan. You are basically traveling to a destination far away in time and no knowledge of how you intend to survive. Our lives can drastically change ten to twenty years out. We need to prepare for it.

The article also says, *you're less likely to budget if you earn less than $75,000* and *there are 1.9 billion open credit cards in the United States.* No matter if you make $20K, $50K, $100K, or over $200K, you must budget because money doesn't last forever. We also need to monitor our credit card activity. Budgeting and monitoring your credit cards go hand in hand. We need to build budgeting into our normal routine and make it a habit. We need to control our spend, especially when we are on the verge of failure. Today, we have many challenges in society with people not being able to control their spend. Priorities are not where they should be and that is when people get into financial trouble.

There are plenty of free resources on the internet that provide great financial information worth looking into. A few of my favorites include *CNN Markets, Forbes Money, Market Watch,* and *Investopedia.* The more we know, the better our decision making becomes. This is why it is important to learn about money. Money is an influence on people everywhere. Think about any decision you've made and ask yourself, would the decision you made be different if money was not a factor? For most decisions, money will be a factor and have some influence on the outcome of that decision. We must keep in mind that the internet also has a lot of bad advice too, so we need to have good judgment. Basically, does it make sense? Does it sound too good to be true? We need to be suspicious and make sure we are not buying into trickery.

For one-year, I wrote blogs for my own website called www.civilaccomplishment.com. The focus of the site was to generate discussion around success at all levels. First, I wanted to share useful information to those who wanted to improve their financial situation. A large piece of becoming successful is establishing expectations and creating plans to meet those expectations. In other words, define your goals and create a roadmap to reach your goals in a timely manner.

Over the course of one year, I published 247 blogs on www.civilaccomplishment.com. I talked about financial planning, opportunities to save money, managing your own business, climbing the corporate ladder, ways to be a better presenter and much-much more. I had a few followers. The website did not generate a cent for me but did cost me $140 for the website service and domain name. During this time in my life, I did not have much time to spare and was spread too thin. Since my blog was a nonessential activity and was costing me money, I made the decision to discontinue the website. I have no regrets in starting or ending the website. Over the course of the year writing blogs, I learned a lot because I was constantly researching topics I was writing about. I forced myself to become the expert on the materials I was writing about.

In thinking about *the average American household having $132,529 worth of debt,* it can be very daunting. This amount of debt can be frightening for most people. Then there are other people who do not seem to care. Let's remember the $132,529 figure is an average, so there are people with less debt and others with more debt. Debt can be unavoidable at times, but we must realize we can take measures to reduce damages caused by debt. Before we get into the weeds of understanding the intricacies of debt, we need to step back and look at the bigger picture. There are things in this world that we can control and things that we simply cannot. We will need to worry about the things we have control over. The other uncontrollable factors do need to be taken into consideration but looked at from a different viewpoint.

A straightforward example I have for an uncontrollable event is, your home gets hit by a tornado. There is nothing you can really do about 'acts of God'. However, you can purchase insurance to mitigate the financial risk of an act of God. You cannot stop a tornado but can put controls in place to help with the financial burden caused by the natural disaster. You can also reduce the risk of being impacted by a natural disaster by living in an area that does not have increased risk for natural disasters. This could be forest fires in Northern California, tornadoes in the Great Plains Tornado Belt, or Hurricanes on the coast of Florida. We are accountable for understanding the risks in our life and making sure we have a plan in case those risks become reality. To understand risks, we must do a risk assessment.

There are two factors we need to consider in doing a risk assessment. They are likelihood and severity. Likelihood is the probability an event will occur. Severity is the seriousness or impact if that event does occur. We can use a *Risk Assessment Table* to determine how much of a risk something is. Let's say the risk you are assessing is the tornado. We would rate severity a '5'. If you live in New Jersey, you'd rate likelihood a '1'. This would give you a '5' in the *Risk Assessment Table*. In our table, we would only be concerned about risks resulting in '8' or higher – see shaded areas. This would mean for a tornado with a severity level of '5', you'd need to hit a likelihood level of at least '2'. If you did live in the Great Plains Tornado Belt, then you should be concerned.

Risk Assessment Table

		Likelihood				
		1	**2**	**3**	**4**	**5**
Severity	**1**	1	2	3	4	5
	2	2	4	6	8	10
	3	3	6	9	12	15
	4	4	8	12	16	20
	5	5	10	15	20	25

The *Risk Assessment Table* can be used for any risk assessment. Just keep in mind, it is a subjective tool and not exact. The major reason to use this tool is to set criteria around what is an acceptable risk and not an acceptable risk. If the risk is acceptable, then no actions are required. If the risk is not acceptable, you would need to take action to mitigate the risk. In the case of the tornado, you would want to either move away from the area where tornados are likely to occur or get good homeowners' insurance that covers tornados.

Risk assessments can be done for natural disasters, potential health issues, car troubles, home appliance malfunctions, and so on. Most of what I just mentioned would fall under the uncontrollable category. It's much better to prepare for risks before they come to fruition. Once a problem arises, you may have very little time to react, forcing you to make decisions on the fly. With little time to gather information, you will have limited knowledge to form an effective game plan. You do not need to have a formal documented plan but should have at minimum a backup plan in mind. Let's say a tree falls on your house. Do you know who to call to? Do you have somewhere else to stay? Will your insurance provider cover costs? These are the types of questions that need to be answered prior to the incident.

If you have trees near your home, then your likelihood rating may be a '3' or '4'. If these are large trees, then your severity rating may also be a '3' or '4'. This would put you in the risk rating range of '9' to '16'. Since this is higher than '8', then you would need to have a plan in place to mitigate risk. If you are just starting to use the **Risk Assessment Table**, then I'd recommend beginning slow. Assessing risk for every possible scenario would take too much time and is not necessary. Start out with the bigger items that you see as bigger risks. Schedule a quick risk assessment review as part of your financial review. The financial review will be discussed in a later chapter.

Now, we can look at the controllable risks and these can be a bit more complicated if we let our emotions get the best of us. Whenever emotion is involved, things can get more complicated. As an example, you get some extra cash and you purchase a new car, even though you have a perfectly good working car nearly paid off. We must realize emotion plays a large role in our purchases. Even though we may have realized purchasing a new car was not right for us financially, our emotions told us to purchase it anyways.

Imagine, a few months pass and you are tight on money because you purchased this new car and ignored other financial factors. Not only are you stuck with payments on this new car, much of those payments are going to interest. Only a few dollars each month go to the principle on your loan. Additionally, other bills are piling up and you are using credit cards to manage them. More interest is accumulating. All of this could have been avoided if you decided to be patient and not purchase a new car, but the temptation was too strong. This is very common and a big reason many people go further into debt. As human-beings, we naturally want things now and have a difficult time waiting for the appropriate time to purchase those things. Our emotions often get the best of us, which is something we need to control.

Controllable events are identified as any event you have control over such as purchasing a new car. Basically, any sort of purchase you make is considered a controllable event. The fact that you are procuring a product and have a choice, makes it 100% controllable. We know food is necessary to live and we also know food is not normally free. We must purchase food. However, the brand, type, quantity, and place we purchase is our decision. If you go to Whole Foods, then you are probably going to spend much more than if you went to Aldi. These are decisions you have control over.

Awareness of your financial situation today is extremely important. Awareness of your goals for the future is equally as important. In my earlier years, money management was not a normal topic at the dinner table, and this is common for most families. The first time I was introduced to the topic of money management was my junior year in high school when I took a class called, *money management*. The teacher of this class was Coach Lancetta. He was the head football coach for my high school at the time and was very respectable.

Coach Lancetta covered quite a bit that year in money management, but what stands out most was his emphasis on current events and the stock market. Every week we were responsible for writing a summary on at least one current event focused on money from the newspaper. I quickly realized it was crucial to pay attention to the economy, interest rates, stock market trends, and so on. These are the types of things we need to consider when making financial decisions in our life. Prior to getting into Coach Lancetta's money management class, I never realized this.

Another lesson Coach Lancetta taught us was on 401(k) and mutual funds. Every several years your 401(k) should double. During the beginning when your 401(k) funds are lower, the doubling is not as great. In your later years when your 401(K) is larger, the doubling is more significant. Coach Lancetta made a point to say the longer you can keep your money in the 401(k), the more impactful the doubling will be. He also stressed the importance of beginning a 401(k) as early as possible because the longer you have money in there, the more return you will gain.

Another fun activity we did in my high school money management class was investing in the stock market. We did not use real money, which may have been a good thing for many of my classmates who did not select good stocks to trade. At the start of the semester, Coach Lancetta allowed each group of three to invest $50,000 in the stock market. Each day we would trade stocks and report back to Coach Lancetta on a weekly basis. My group was very successful by turning $50,000 into $150,000. This activity required us to research the companies we were investing in. It required us to predict the future of these companies based on the clues from our research. Coach Lancetta was very impressed with our team's return on investment. However, I am not confident I could generate such a great return on investment with real money. I would also not be willing to use my personal money for some of the risks we took.

Although I was interested in money management, I was more interested in science. At the same time, I was also interested in psychology. It was during my junior year in high school when I took a psychology course, which was only for seniors. Somehow, I was able to take this senior level course my junior year of high school. It made me feel smart and gave other senior students in the class the illusion that I was smarter than I actually was. This psychology class was interesting enough to motivate me to major in psychology my first year in college. Later on, in my college career, I would change my major from psychology to biochemistry.

Transitioning from psychology to biochemistry was not easy, but I knew it had to be done. From a young age of 12 or 13 years old, my mother would take me to Edmund Scientific, which was a supplier of science stuff. They had chemicals, glassware for laboratories, animals to dissect, science classes for kids, and so much more. Each time my mother would take me, she would buy me something. At home, my father built me a room in the basement for my science experiments. I would spend a considerable amount of time in that lab trying to be a scientist, even though I did not know what I was doing. The reason I did not immediately start off as a science major in college is because I was not confident enough. My high school grades were a disaster and I have no one to blame, but myself. This will be discussed later on.

Jumping ahead to my early college years, my father and I started a business fabricating custom equipment for the agricultural industry. This was a trade my father worked in his entire life. My father worked the majority of his career for a fortune 500 company in the factory, corporate engineering, and maintenance department. He has several patents and has been a key player for the teams he has worked on. He brings vast manufacturing experience and technical expertise in the areas of equipment, processing, and packaging. My father is someone people go to when they cannot figure out a problem. He is someone who makes the impossible, possible!

A year or so before starting our own company building equipment, I worked with my father on some side construction jobs. We would remodel small offices, which included tearing walls down, putting new walls up, spackling, painting, installation of windows, showers, toilets, and anything else you can think of. I have always considered myself to have good work ethic. Working hard has always been the expectation when it came to physical labor. Expectations around school were a little bit unclear from time to time. We can also get into this a bit later.

There was one blueberry farmer who went to the same church as us that asked my father to build him a stainless-steel conveyor for his packing house. This was the start of our machine shop in 2008. This first piece of equipment was built out of my parents' two-car garage, which was in a residential area. We did not want the neighbors complaining, so we kept the garage doors closed while we worked on the machine. I had no prior experience in equipment fabrication, so it was all new to me. At this point, I did not even know how to weld. My father took me under his wing and taught me about machining, welding, fabricating, design, engineering, and the list goes on. All of this information has benefited me greatly later down the road.

Since I was 90 miles away at college, I would drive 2-hours back home to work with my dad at our machine shop each weekend. When I say machine shop, I am talking about my parents' garage where we had a drill press, small welder, and some other tools to build equipment. In the earlier days of our fabrication business, it was very difficult to complete projects quickly with the lack of tools available to us. As we generated more money, we purchased better tools and eventually moved our business to a larger building. It became necessary once we purchased a lathe, mill, sand blaster, and so on. We needed more space to store our equipment and building materials. Not only did we need the extra space, but our neighbors were beginning to get curious. At one point, I was polishing a machine in my parents' garage, when the buffing wheel unhinged. This buffing wheel shot through the air towards the bottom of my parents' driveway where our neighbor Sam was walking his dog. I can still remember the confused, yet perturbed look on his face. I guess I'd be upset too if I almost got hit by a buffing wheel when I least expected it.

In addition to working in the machine shop with my father, I also kept the financial records. My father was not as enthusiastic for record keeping as I was. He was also not as organized, and I could see things getting messy if he kept the records. My responsibilities eventually expanded to project manager, writing invoices and quotes, strategic planning, and so on. I was pretty good at the office work. I needed to make sure I was getting the engineering piece in case I had to design and fabricate alone one day. My biggest worry was not having the support of my father because initially he was the brains of our operation. Later on, I contributed more both mentally and physically. After a year or so of learning about building equipment from my father, I was able to contribute more value to our company.

After college, I moved back home full-time and started working as a chemist for a startup pharmaceutical company. Due to a low salary, no medical coverage or retirement benefits, and my lack of perceived future at that company, I continued working hard with my father at our business on nights and weekends. I spent three years at the startup company and then moved to a consumer packaged goods company as a maintenance technician.

My background working with my father in our machine shop made me a good fit for the maintenance role. This lasted 6 months until I found a position in the company's packaging department as a packaging engineer. Before this, I applied to countless jobs in and outside of the organization. I applied for a chemist role, food technologist role, procurement role, and lab technician role to name just a few roles I applied for.

I did not have any formal training as a packaging engineer, but my chemistry background was useful to one of the larger packaging projects during that time. I spent 6 years in the packaging department. During this time, I earned my master's degree from Michigan State University in packaging. Since my employer was offering to give me a full reimbursement to get my graduate degree, I simply could not say no. I did not have to pay one-cent, which makes it much sweeter. Shortly after receiving my master's degree, I transitioned into another role in Supply Chain. At the time, I felt I took away all I could have from the packaging department in terms of learning. It was my time to move.

To recap, I've spent a bunch of time in school earning a bachelor's and master's degree, worked 3 years as a chemist in a startup pharmaceutical company, 6 months in maintenance, 6 years in packaging as a packaging engineer, and many more years in Supply Chain in various functions. Throughout this entire time, I was working in parallel with my father at our machine shop building equipment. So why is this important?

Throughout my many years as a student and professional in the industry, I learned money management is extremely important to your success. It does not matter if you are making over $250,000 or earning less than $20,000 per year. Money management is critical to your financial future. Typically, those with larger salaries are more likely to know how to manage their money. Much of the time, it is the individuals with lower salaries that need more help in understanding how to manage money. For instance, the article titled, *10 Statistics About the Money Habits of The Average American* has #5 on the list as, *you're less likely to budget if you earn less than $75,000 per year.*

In the lower salary ranges, budgets become even more important because you have less room for error. At the opposite end of the spectrum, just because you make a lot of money also does not mean you should not have a budget. When I was making much less money as a chemist, I opted to live at home with my parents and get rid of my student loan debt quickly. If I moved out like most of my other friends during that time, I would not have had the ability to pay down student loan debt as quickly and would have ended up paying much more interest to the bank. We need to make sure we are stretching our money as far as possible. Interest, fees, or any other charges are not going to principle become our enemy.

For clarification, **I am not an accountant or any type of certified financial advisor**. However, I do have personal experiences I'd like to share with others to make their lives easier. My hope is to inspire others to become more engaged in managing their money *effectively*. I would like others to gain control of their financial situation and have the ability to retire earlier on in life. It is highly unlikely that money will just drop out of the sky into your hands and allow you to become independently wealthy. It is our job to take accountability for our own financial situation, create a goal for the future, create the direction to achieve the goal, and work towards achieving that goal. Those who have done well for themselves in this world, have done just that. They have done well for themselves and this was intentional. As a former manager once told me, *hope is not a plan.*

At this point in my life, my number one financial priority is to remove all debt. This means my mortgage, wife's student loans, and wife's car loan. We have two children under the age of two years old, a cat, and dog. We live in a middle-class suburban community in New Jersey. We are a very happy family! My fear is not being able to support my family, and this is why I focus so strongly on financial stability. I am taking the opportunity today while I am still healthy and strong to build my financial portfolio in case some day, I am not able to do so. Life can provide you unexpected challenges when you least expect it. Much of the time, we are faced with challenges when we are most vulnerable. I do not want to wait until that day to realize I need financial stability for my family. I cease the opportunity to capture financial stability when I am willing and capable.

In this book, I will give you guidance on how to get debts paid quickly. As a disclaimer, I want to make sure you know there is nothing magical about it. There are no clever tricks to paying off your debts faster. There are a few things you should know when you are willingly taking on a new debt, such as a mortgage. For example, make sure there are no early payoff penalties because you will want to pay off your debt as early as possible to reduce the overall interest you pay. Additionally, you will never want to be late on a payment because late fees are just a ridiculous way to waste money. These are the types of things we need to watch out for. I will not be able to provide each infinitesimal detail, but can provide a strategic view that should help you make better financial decisions.

First of all, your goal should be to get out of debt. This is your number one financial priority until you achieve 0% debt. Once you achieve this goal, you will then set goals to build up funds for your retirement. It all sounds lame and I'm completely aware of that, but is it lame when you retire earlier than all of your friends? Or is it lame when you have tons of money you can spend on a new fancy car and pay cash for it? I think those types of things are super cool. At the end of the day, if you have more control over your cash, you have more control over your life. I want to know I can provide my children with whatever they need. It would pain me to say 'no' because I simply did not have the funds to support their field trip or plans to play hockey. When we have children, we all know it is going to be expensive, so why not prepare as early as possible?

The other really neat thing about these methods I am going to talk about is, you don't need to be a millionaire to succeed at using them. Electronic spreadsheets such as Microsoft Excel are definitely a must. You could track your expenses using a pen and notepad, but that can become messy quick. In my opinion, Microsoft Excel is one of the greatest programs ever created and keeps getting better. And no, Bill Gates does not pay me a cent to endorse Microsoft Excel. Throughout this book I am going to provide tables, graphs, and diagrams to illustrate my points. I am going to provide as many tools as possible to help you succeed in your future endeavors in the financial world. I would also encourage you to reach out to me directly with any questions, concerns, or comments.

Another portion will be getting to know your bank and credit cards for tracking purposes. Monthly, I record my savings, checking, credit card debts, utility bills, mortgage, and so on. This helps me become aware of my progress towards my goals. Trends can be useful in knowing what to expect each year. When we are thinking about budgets for the year, we can use yearly trends to help us determine if we can add costs for the upcoming year. Maybe you would like to install a new inground swimming pool or hire a landscaper. You can review your year to year expenses and estimate whether you will have any money left over for the upcoming year. This method of monthly review also allows us to catch any fraudulent activity your bank or credit card company did not catch.

Lastly, I must mention commitment is crucial to your success. Without commitment to these efforts, you are setting yourself up for failure before you ever begun. It cannot be 25%, 50%, or even 75% commitment. It must be 100% commitment to guarantee you will be successful. If you are able to consistently review your financials monthly and keep your financial goals top of mind, you are more likely to succeed. If you are able to bring your spouse or partner into the effort and align, you are even more likely to succeed. A consistent 100% commitment throughout the entire lifecycle of your goal is an absolute requirement for success. I do not believe in luck when it comes to financial success, nor should you.

As Coach Lancetta once said, *it is better to make money by working for it, then hope to win the lottery by chance. Work guarantees you a paycheck. The lottery does not!*

A co-worker of mine was talking to me early one morning and brought up the idea that successful people are not usually only talented in one area. He strongly believed successful people are usually talented in multiple areas. This is quite the generalization, but I wanted to further explore this idea. My brain scanned for successful people I knew to see if there were any correlations between being successful and being multi-talented. One by one, I thought of close friends who are successful in their field.

There is my friend Jonathan Squibb AKA Super Squibb, who is a three-time Wing Bowl champion. Wing Bowl is a competitive eating event in Philadelphia, which had over 20,000 attendees each year. The participants in the competition eat chicken wings as fast as they possibly can to win whatever the big prize was for that year. Sometimes it was $20,000 in cash, a new car, and occasionally both cash and car. Jon ate 203, 238, and 255 chicken wings in Wing Bowl 27, 28, and 29, respectively. In college, Jonathan rowed for the Rutgers Crew Team and was one of their better rowers. After college, Jonathan did very well for himself as an accountant at Price Waterhouse Cooper. Jon has always been very competitive and excels at mostly everything he gets his hands on. Here was one clear example of someone who is successful and multi-talented.

Then, I thought of another close friend of mine, Dan Pope who is a physical therapist, but not just any physical therapist. This guy has been an inspiration to many since he first participated in sports from a young age. I first met

Dan in high school and can still remember the day he did 35 consecutive pull-ups in gym class to set my high school's pull-up record. Since then he has achieved being a Division 1 Collegiate Pole Vaulter at Rutgers University, National Champion Strongman multiple times, earned a Doctor of Physical Therapy, written for countless magazines and websites, and the list goes on. In addition to all of these great accomplishments, which you can read about on his website www.fitnesspainfree.com, he is a phenomenal businessman and great friend. Dan is also asked to speak at events internationally to educate athletes on physical health. Here is another example of someone who is successful and multi-talented.

One last personal close friend and favorite of mine, Mike Baturin who I've known since I was 12-years old. First of all, Mike is incredibly genuine and has great intentions. I've spent a great deal of time with Mike during my high school years playing in the same rock band, hanging out at the movies, going to the mall, and being in the same classes in school. Mike is a smart critical thinker and problem solver. He has worked extremely hard in the field of information technology and has gained much recognition and respect for it. In our group of friends, he is known as our personal tech guru. If he does not know about a technology or application, it probably doesn't exist. One of his best traits in my opinion is his sense of humor. Within 10 seconds of meeting Mike, he will make you laugh and cry at the same time. Yet another example of someone who is successful and multi-talented.

These are just three examples of successful people who are also multi-talented. I agree with my co-worker that it helps to have multiple talents in different areas. As they say, don't keep all of your eggs in one basket. As I continue to think about it, I am more convinced only lucrative talents contribute to your financial stability. Your talents need to generate a profit. An individual who is a great sculptor and vocalist may not necessarily generate significant income in this lifetime solely because of those talents. There have been plenty of amazing artists who died poor such as Johann Sebastian Bach and Edgar Allan Poe. A key takeaway here is, if you want to have money in this lifetime, focus on finding a career that will pay you in this lifetime.

Fortunately, I realized this early on in my college career, which is why I switched from psychology to biochemistry. To make decent money in the field of psychology, I would have had to earn a doctorate degree. I worked at a medical school earlier on in my college career and was told by psychologists with doctorates that they did not earn as much as they thought they would. After researching the job market, I knew I'd have more opportunities with a degree in biochemistry, which did prove true. I was able to join a pharmaceutical startup company as a chemist. I also got my foot in the door in the packaging department at a fortune 500 company because of my chemistry background.

Although I did enjoy psychology, I knew I needed to set myself up for success financially. When thinking about a job, we should be focused on three areas – position, location, and salary. The order of importance is personal preference. Obviously, we do need to find the job interesting and enjoyable. We also need to make sure the job is in a location that works for you and your family. You would need to make sure the salary is adequate to support you and your family. The salary also needs to be appropriate for the job and level of responsibility you are taking on. If you are a vice president in your company, then you would expect to get paid much more than if you were entry level or mid-senior level. A vice president will have much more responsibility and expected to provide greater results than someone at a lower level.

I would like to take a second to travel back in time to my younger years in elementary school through high school. There were always the typical math, science, English, and history type classes. When it came time to pick a career, I never felt the school gave great guidance on real jobs. This may be why I decided to major in psychology my freshman year of college. My guidance counselor in high school called me into her office one day to discuss my future. I told her I wanted to go to a 4-year college to earn a degree in psychology. Based on my grades, she did not think I'd get into a good 4-year college. Based on my grades, I don't think she thought I'd amount to much in life. Fast forward and I was at my local community college my freshman year trying to earn grades good enough to get into a 4-year college. I guess my guidance counselor could predict the future to some extent.

Since I did not get into any of the schools I applied to, I felt ashamed. It is difficult to see your friends go on to good schools and you are left behind to attend your local community college. I really wanted to live in a dorm away from home and get the full college experience. This is an experience I rarely think about because it doesn't make me feel good about myself. Although it provokes negative feelings, it did impact my life in a positive way. For starters, I knew I needed to fix my priorities. My number one priority needed to be school. I needed to get better grades at the community college, so I could apply to a 4-year college and get accepted. This would require more studying and less adventures with my friends. The embarrassment of not getting into a 4-year school was enough motivation for me. I knew it was not too late to turn this boat around.

I often reflect on my years in high school and ask myself, where did I go wrong? Why was I not the valedictorian of my class? If not valedictorian, why was I not the top 10% of students in my class? Today, I see I am a pretty smart guy, but back then I acted like a fool. There is no prettier way to say it. Even a lot of my friends thought I was a little dumb from time to time, which did not stop me from having fun. My father said I was not challenged enough, which I am not sure that's entirely true. I would like to agree to save face, but I think there is something else. I think my interests were not aligned well with the curriculum at my school. I did end up taking an IQ test and ended up with a *129*. Based on these results, I would be deemed as *'**superior intelligence**'*. This makes me feel better about myself.

I was never a huge history fan. I was never really a huge literature fan. The same goes for many of my other classes, but I did enjoy math and science. Although I enjoyed these classes, I was never confident enough to achieve success in the classroom. For starters, I was always told at home to do my best, which was my license to justify my poor grades. I would say I was trying my hardest and doing my best, even though I really was not. In reality, I should have been held accountable for my poor marks. If I could go back in time and talk to my younger-self, I would stare him straight in the eyes and say *you have no excuse*. My brain was fully functional and capable of straight As. My priorities were not straight, and I ended up suffering for it later on in college.

I was under the impression the only way to study was to memorize the learning materials. I learned this tactic from my brother, which is most definitely not the best way to learn information. By repeating definitions over and over again, you are not setting yourself up for success in your school career. Even if you can remember the information for your first exam, you may not be able to remember the materials months later for a cumulative exam that covers all materials you were supposed to learn since day one of that class. The most effective studying techniques for me include using visual aids and associating the terms with something I am more familiar with. I've used this outside of school to remember people's names, birthdays, anniversaries, details about certain people, and so on. As one example, I can remember my parents' wedding anniversary because it is one day after my birthday. I can also remember my friend Tyrone's birthday because it is six days after my birthday. Dates are always difficult to remember when you have nothing tangible to relate them to.

Fast forward once again to my college years. Since I did not fully understand the basics of math, I needed to work twice as hard, especially when I got into the higher-level calculus classes. Without knowing the basic fundamentals of algebra and trigonometry, I was doomed from the start. I needed to understand the building blocks for calculus to have a fighting chance to succeed. Similarly, I needed to relearn all the basics of science again before I could truly understand the higher-level science courses. I paid for my lack of accountability in high school by needing to devote more time and effort in college. In high school, I did not know the proper ways to study and I did not take the time to figure it out. By doing poorly and saying I was doing my best, I was not pressured further to do better. Nobody looked at why I was not succeeding or how I could improve.

I can distinctively remember having a rough start in my biology 101, chemistry 101, physics 101, and calculus I courses, to name a few. It would seem as if I'd be fine because these are introductory type courses. In reality, there was an expectation that you would know some basics from your high school classes. I did not pay attention in these courses in high school and I'm certain I did not even take physics or calculus in high school. To succeed in these courses, I sought extra help outside from professors, teacher assistants, peer students, and tutors. If someone was willing to help me, I was going to accept the help. I was also not afraid to ask for extra help because I did not want to fail. This was one of the main reasons I was able to catch up and succeed in these courses.

In college, since I stayed proactive in seeking extra help, it showed my professors I was not willing to give up. They could see I was truly doing my best to achieve acceptable grades. If there were times I was between a C and B or B and A, they'd usually give me an extra point or two to get me to the higher grade. I learned to be more vocal and ask more questions. As time went by, I cared a little bit less about what others would say about me. I also learned that *others probably have the same questions as you and are just not asking them.* School is a place of learning and questions must be asked. It helps the professors gauge where their students are. If no questions are asked during lectures, then a professor could assume their students understand everything. Then the exam comes, and many students fail. This proves there was a disconnect. I did not want to be a part of this disconnect. At the same time, I was not as serious as I could have been.

Many years after being a professional and going back to graduate school, things were much different. I've been out in the field for a while working with professional people. These were people who expected to win and did not accept excuses for failures. They did exceptionally well in school because they took it very seriously. I've learned from them to also be serious about school. I also did not want to look foolish by performing poorly in graduate school because my employer was paying, which means they'd see all my grades. Due to my transformation, I finished graduate school with nearly a 4.0 GPA. This was phenomenal and shows me I was capable all along of doing much better.

Besides being more serious about my schooling the second time around, I also had new sets of skills and a better understanding of how to be effective. In the real world we do not always have adequate time to complete projects. Due to these circumstances, we quickly become efficient and effective in all we do. Using these skills, I was able to complete school work faster with greater effectiveness. In listening to professor's lectures, I'd listen for the items they'd deem most important. This is where I'd spend most of my time studying because I knew it would be on the exam. I also made sure I would devote 100% of my attention to my school work when I worked on it for maximum effectiveness. I eliminated all distractions while working on school assignments and studying. There were times in college when I'd study while watching TV. This is a very poor habit.

Similar to school, in the workplace we are asked to set goals and achieve those goals within a set amount of time. This becomes challenging to many because so many of us get bored, discouraged, or unfocused over a lengthy period of time. I have illustrated a starting point and end point with a person standing near the start. This is an illustration to show where we start in the beginning of a new project. Defining the start and end can be relatively easy in comparison to identifying the challenges that may occur along the way.

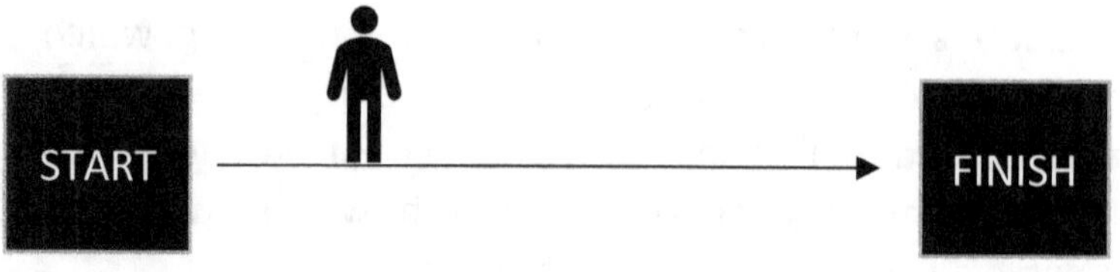

As we learn more about the project, we learn it will be more challenging than we first perceived. Now, the illustration has obstacles between the start and finish, which can be discouraging. We may not be adding more time to the timeline to compensate for these new challenges, which can be an issue. During my high school years, I may have been slightly aware of my starting point. I would not say I was completely clear on my end point. I also did not think about the challenges I was faced with too much, if at all.

If I had sat down and mapped out the start, finish, and challenges, things would have been dramatically different. Just having the awareness of my situation would have helped me get my creative juices flowing. This process would have pushed me into problem solving mode and made me realize, yes- I need to fix something. It would have helped me better prepare for challenges on my path forward. If I only knew I would not get accepted to a 4-year college because of my poor grades, I may have performed a little better. The thought of embarrassment and disappointment alone should have motivated me to do better. If we do not identify where our finish line is, then we will have very little control over how we get there. We would not have a meaningful purpose for our efforts.

The main point here is, we need to see the whole picture. Only knowing your starting point is not enough. Only knowing your end point is not enough. You must determine your starting point, end point, and understand the challenges along the way. I cannot emphasize this point enough. Without a map detailing your path forward, you are going to have trouble indicating when you have achieved what you set out to do. You will not know how many years of work to anticipate or the amount of work required to achieve your goals. In life, I fear most ***not knowing*** because uncertainty simply frightens me. When I am provided details about the future, I become more comfortable because I am able to make decisions based on those details. I would know what to expect and this calms my nerves.

We need to take a step back and make sure we have a reasonable plan in place to guide us and help us achieve our goals. Once you do that, it is time to roll up your sleeves, and get dirty. Your job is to execute your plan and reach your goals. This requires work. The most challenging part for me is building the strategy to execute my goals. Once the strategy portion is done, the work is the easy part. You may be more strategic and have an easier time building strategy than executing the work. For most of us, we are required to perform both functions in our personal lives. I also think it is good to carry out both functions because it makes us well-rounded. We need to be strategic thinkers and have the ability to perform tactical duties.

During my time in packaging and supply chain, I have participated in an effort to help children in the local community learn about different professional careers. These were urban children living in poverty who did not have the same opportunities as some other children from more affluent areas. A 5th grade class from the local elementary school was selected to participate in this program. A presentation from each department across the organization was given to the students to help them understand what opportunities are out there. There were many departments that presented including marketing, sales, human resources, information technology, finance, engineering, procurement, and packaging to name a few. I presented on the packaging materials to the students.

My presentation consisted of an introduction to myself and how I got into packaging. I went over the different activities packaging engineers do during a normal week and also had them participate in a packaging challenge. Throughout my presentation the students would ask many questions. I could tell they were interested in learning about packaging. I also realized my enthusiasm helped them feel more excited about it. There were some other presenters with less enthusiasm, which did not help the students get excited about their department. At the end of the day, I loved it and felt I was impacting these kids' lives for the better. My win is not them becoming packaging engineers. My win is opening their minds up to new opportunities that they did not know existed or were even possible career opportunities.

This program to educate local students on different cross-functional roles is a fantastic idea. These are the types of activities that should be replicated at all schools because not everyone should be a policeman, psychologist, doctor, or electrician. Not that these are bad jobs. There are so many lucrative career opportunities out there that are both interesting and satisfying. If somebody presented this information to me in my younger years, I could have possibly found my way to a role I enjoyed easier. This information could have helped me find my end point, thus giving me something to work towards.

In addition to providing young students in middle school and high school with possible careers outside the normal selection, let the students know about potential salaries. Give the students an idea of the cost of living and why inflation is an important factor to consider. There needs to be a course devoted for career planning and goal setting. In all of my younger years from elementary school to high school, there was only one class that touched on this. This was money management, which was discussed in chapter 1. There needs to be more of this because it is tangible and real. Most of us are not going to succeed by knowing the third president of the United States was Thomas Jefferson. A shift in focus should go to the more useful information. A review of historical type information could be useful, but priority should be on how to make students successful in their careers.

Education is a very large portion of being successful. We need to constantly improve ourselves to advance. Promotions do not typically happen because you are doing the same thing over and over again. In fact, doing the same thing over and over again, and doing it well, may actually convince your managers to keep you in that current role. Managers typically do not like to find a replacement, especially when the person they have today is doing a great job. Replacements require onboarding that take up management's time. Education and training can help you become more qualified for larger roles. This is crucial to your career growth.

At this point, I have told you a little bit about my background and the purpose of this book. I have also given some perspective on what makes someone successful. Although, there is not one formula that makes someone a guaranteed success, there are certain ingredients you will need. The first ingredient I'll talk about is **commitment**. Some could argue commitment is the most crucial ingredient. It is the ingredient that will keep you on task throughout the entire process of achieving your goals.

A tool I use to remind myself daily of my commitment to my goals is my journal. I have been keeping this journal since June 15, 2005. I started the journal to track my progress towards my goals in life. I write daily in this journal using a blue or black pen. Never pencil! After several months, I go back and type up the journal entries into an electronic word document. This helps me remember what I set out to do several months prior. It helps me understand if I'm on track or falling behind. If I am falling behind, I can course correct to get back on track. My journal entries have proven to be useful for many years. This tool reminds me I must keep myself accountable and stay committed. Nobody else will do this for me.

Going back into my earlier journal entries, the thoughts and opinions were of someone who was immature. If I went back in time and asked if I thought I was immature, I would say 'no'. It was during a time in my life when I was surrounded with mostly immaturity. My focus was not on building a career or starting a family. My focus was more on partying and having a good time. I felt some peer pressure to be someone who was fun. If my peers expected me to focus on my career, perhaps then I would have focused more on building my career. I cannot blame my friends for my lack of maturity. At the end of the day, my close friends and I ended up being successful.

When I was a freshman in college, I did not have a solid life plan. This was a time when I was majoring in psychology, excited about girls, and just wanted to have fun. I did take my college studies more seriously than my high school years, but still not serious enough to get straight A's. During the start of my journal entry I was finishing up my first year at community college and was preparing to transfer to a 4-year school. My goals were not very clear at this point, but I did know I needed to document my thoughts and I am glad I did.

My journal writing actually began as part of an assignment in a class I took called, psychology of personality. My professor had everyone start a journal as an assignment. At the end of each week on Friday it was required we submit it to the professor to read over the weekend. She commented to me one day how she loved reading my journal. She said it was very funny and whenever she was having a rough day, she could read it and feel better. At the end of the semester I never did get my journal back from my professor. The journal I keep today that I started on June 15, 2005 is not the same journal I started in my psychology class. I am always curious to see what I wrote in that journal. What was so funny to my professor? It has been over 15 years, which explains why I cannot remember what I wrote.

As years went by, I can see my writings have improved. My thoughts and objectives became clearer. It probably took a good 5 years to realize results matter. For the longest time I thought doing work was good enough. I thought my effort was what really counted, but in the real world that is not always true. It is the results you produce that really matter. In college, even though I studied quite a bit, if my grades were bad, why did it matter? Effort or amount of work do not always translate to results as a 1:1 ratio. This speaks to effectiveness of your methods. If I am studying 40 hours per week and not earning acceptable grades, I need to rethink my method of studying. Simply, something needs to change. However, this was not my mindset during my college years.

During my high school and college years, I did not have the sense to understand why I was not succeeding. I was not mature enough to face why I performed poorly. It was not until college when I started getting extra help. As I read through old journal entries and time progresses forward, I can see my maturity level increasing. As my maturity increased, I started making better decisions. There are decisions I made at the end of college that I would have never known to make during high school or the beginning of college. There are decisions I made in my professional career that I would not have known to make as a student. These are the types of things my journal allows me to reflect on.

To illustrate the effectiveness of studying and why it matters, I created two boxes. The first box contains what you studied – square, circle, and triangle. The second box contains what was actually on the exam – square and triangle. Of course, these are just representative symbols of topics that you may have studied and what is on the exam. Imagine each topic or shape, takes you 2 hours to master. If the circle was never going to be on the exam, what is the point of using time to study the circle? More time can be devoted to the square and/or triangle. This is a type of thinking I did not have during my years as a student.

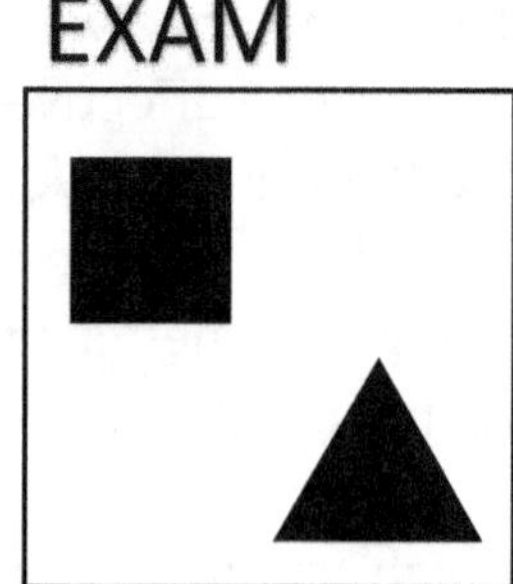

This type of thinking can be applied to our professional careers too. There are some projects we may want to focus on that have a significant impact to the business and other projects that have very little impact. My point here is not to take shortcuts. My point here is to understand what is in scope and put efforts towards the things that count most. This is very important when you are limited on time because you have an overwhelming amount of work that needs to be done. This type of strategic thinking will set you apart from others. Prioritization skills are increasingly important as you climb in your career.

Most of the time in college, I had a packed schedule. A typical semester would be 3 or 4 challenging science classes with an independent study on a specific biochemistry or chemistry topic. One of my final semesters in college was biochemistry II, senior seminar, analytical chemistry II, physical chemistry II, and a chemistry independent study. Each of the biochemistry, analytical chemistry, and physical chemistry courses had lab work, which took 3-4 hours extra per class per week. That is an extra 9-12 hours per week in the lab. There would be more time required outside of the lab to write the lab reports. These were challenging times and I needed to manage my time wisely. At the time, I studied everything that we talked about and I did not prioritize based on importance. This is one thing that could have helped me become a better student. I did not implement any strategy whatsoever.

Imagine, you have 12 total hours of work to accomplish, but only have capacity for 8 hours. Where are you going to cut out 4 hours of work to fit it into your schedule? It is possible you are overloading yourself and will need to assess your workload. You can prioritize what work you complete as shown in the example with the shapes – square, circle, and triangle. You can also add time by removing activities from outside this category altogether. You may have plans to attend a party or see a concert. You can sacrifice those events and use that time for your work. Of course, this would not be the most favorable option. The purpose of the illustration here is to show that you have 12 blocks or hours, that simply will not fit into the larger block, which represents 8 hours of capacity.

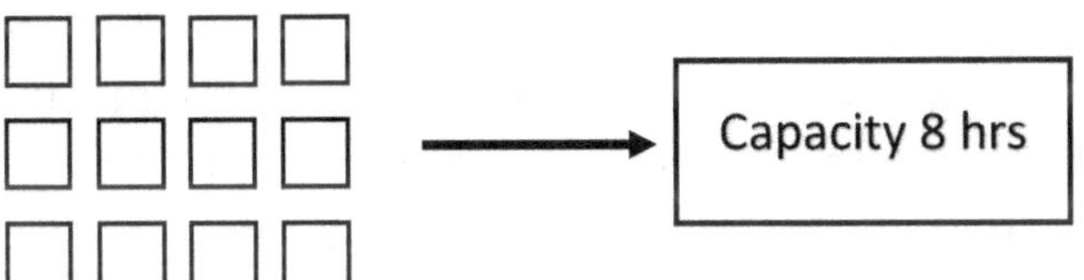

There were nights I did not get to sleep until midnight and the next day I'd wake up at 5 am to continue studying before my first class at 8 am. I can remember every meal being at the library or in my dorm room. I never had a TV because I knew I needed to devote all my time to studying and school assignments. I will confess there were many nights of partying too, which did not help my academic career. Since I did not have a strategy to succeed in school, my studying and partying were all over the place. I truly believe you can have a balanced life in college with both partying and adequate studies. It is just knowing what that mix should be. That is a difficult question to answer.

When we get put in these situations, where we are up to our neck in stress, we cannot think to use any more time on anything, but the work itself. In reality, we need to take a step back and work on an effective strategy to produce results that matter. If I did do this in college, I may have been able to free up a few extra hours per week. Those few extra hours could have been used for sleep, working out at the gym, letting my mind rest, or allowing myself more time for classes that needed extra attention. This would have reduced my stress levels and help me focus on what matters most. Unfortunately, I was never taught this before joining the workforce.

When I read my journal entries now from 2005 to 2009, I sometimes wish I could go back in time and teach my younger self so much. At the same time, I am grateful for the experiences I had, even if I did struggle. When you experience something firsthand, it means so much more. There are parts of my journal I read and am genuinely disappointed in some of the choices I've made. There were times I ate too much, drank too much, didn't go to the gym enough, didn't study enough, and too many others to list here. Society provides endless pressures to younger individuals and those pressures can rapidly mold you into something you are not. Peer pressure can be extreme, especially when you are not fully developed into a mature adult. I can relive those moments every time I open my journal and read about dumb decisions I've made.

Fortunately, I've made more good decisions than bad decisions. Every day we are making decisions, even if you are not aware of it. Waking up and going to school or work is a decision. Trying hard or not, is a decision. Doing what is right or not, is a decision. Eating or not, is a decision. The important thing to remember is, we are accountable for all of our decisions. I was accountable for my decisions in high school and college. I did not do great in high school, so I ended up going to a community college for 1-year, until I could get into a 4-year college. I did not make a strategy for effective studying in college, so my grades suffered. I drank and ate more than I should have, so I gained weight in college.

Yes- peer pressure tempted me to make these poor decisions, but at the end of the day, these were my decisions. Additionally, it was my life and I'd have to live with the outcome of my decisions. If I could have done better in high school, learned more, and did not have to work twice as hard in college to catch up, I would have. If I could have ate better and not had to work twice as hard to get my weight down near the end of college, I would have. Since we realize bad decisions lead to bad outcomes, why don't we just make good decisions? This is the easiest solve of them all, but for some strange reason people are notorious for making bad decisions. It almost feels as if it is our nature to make bad decisions. We also like to laugh when others are making bad decisions, but then we go out and make our own bad decisions.

Bad decisions are super common in the world of finance, especially personal finance. Although I am talking a lot about non-financial stuff, we must realize bad financial decisions are more common than not. I've mentioned earlier the decision to purchase a new car, even though you already have a car that is almost paid off and in working condition. Only this type of decision can come from someone who cannot control themselves, which is most people. Why buy a new car when you have nearly no debt on your current car that works fine? Quite simply, because it's human nature to make bad decisions. And it is our nature to justify our bad decisions with crazy excuses like, my car is going to cost me too much in maintenance soon or the new car is going to save me money on gas.

In reality, you have no data backing that you will save on maintenance costs because you have not yet had any issues with your car breaking. Furthermore, you will save a few hundred dollars each month when your car is paid off and this should be more than enough to cover maintenance fees. Lastly, you are probably not saving more than a few hundred dollars per month on gas, so the no payment on your car is much less than the gas money you are going to save with the new car. Too often we let our emotions persuade us instead of letting the facts control our decisions. In this case, the facts would provide us with data showing us it is simply not smart to purchase a new car.

Bad decisions don't always have to generate a lot of attention and we should realize this. Anytime someone goes out and purchases clothes they cannot afford, that too is a bad decision. Anytime someone goes out and spends a bunch of money on alcohol they cannot afford, that too is a bad decision. Frequent subtle bad decisions will eventually weigh you down. If we are low on cash, should we really be buying useless junk that adds no value to our life? Even if we can afford the alcohol or clothes separately, purchasing both can ultimately put us into a difficult situation. It is important to monitor our expenses, even if you think some of your expenses are negligible. You could be surprised at what the data shows once you view it as a system.

In this chapter, we discussed quite a bit and a broad range of topics. A big take away for you at this point, is to remember to stay committed to your goals and do this any way you know how. For me, it was to write in a journal every day and I am still doing it today. As we progress forward, I'll talk more about my personal experiences and why I chose to do certain things that ended up benefiting me. Much of the information I have today did not come out of a book, but from networking with people. I will further discuss the idea of learning from other people's experiences to benefit you. We do not all need to jump off a cliff to realize it is a poor decision. As important as it is to learn from other peoples' good decisions, it is just as important to learn from their bad decisions too.

I would not consider someone dumb for doing something wrong when they truly did not know it was wrong. I would consider someone dumb for doing something wrong when they knew it was wrong. We have plenty of people driving down a one-way road the wrong way, hoping to get to where they are going a bit faster. This is a risk they are willing to take until they get caught. There are consequences to every poor choice and those consequences need to be examined beforehand. Are you willing to deal with the consequences if you fail and knowing you are making poor decisions? Is the reward worth the risk? These are questions we are going to try to answer in the next several chapters.

At this point, I'd recommend you thinking about how you are going to stay committed to your goals. Are you going to write them in a journal? Are you going to post them somewhere in your house for all to see? Are you going to ask someone you confide in to make sure you don't give up? There are many possibilities to make sure you stay committed to your goals, but at the end of the day, it is your responsibility to hold yourself accountable. This is part of being a mature adult. I learned this later in life. I'd recommend you learn this sooner rather than later.

I have a friend who almost ended up dead in a car crash while being under the influence of alcohol. This was an eye-opening moment in my life because he was very close to me and I did not truly think this could have happened to anyone I knew. Since this did happen to someone I knew, it began making me think, it could happen to me. Maybe not this exact same situation, but maybe something else. My friend clearly did not plan for this tragic event in his life, else he would have tried to prevent it. I know I felt invincible in my younger years, which explains why I did some of the things I did.

In high school, a speaker came in to talk to everyone during one of our school assemblies. This speaker told us to look around the room. He said that not everyone you see today will be alive in a few years based on statistics. This means some of us sitting in that room would be dead in just a few years. This was a very morbid thought. He continued to talk about the risks of overdosing on drugs, car crashes, illnesses, and so on. My friend's near-death experience happened a few years later, while I was a sophomore in college. Upon first hearing the news about my friend's accident, reality did not immediately set in. However, I did think about that speaker from my high school assembly and what he said.

The day after the car crash, I was at my brother's house-warming party, oblivious to my friend's tragic event. My brother and his wife just moved into their new home, so they had a bunch of their friends and family over. My friend who was in the car accident was also invited, but did not show. It was not until later on that evening when I found out that he did not make it because he was in the hospital. Upon first hearing the news from my friend's brother, it did not sound too serious. I asked my friend's brother where my friend was because I hadn't heard from him in a day or so. I also was curious why he missed my brother's party. His brother texted, *brother is in the hospital... car accident.* From this message, I did not think it could have been too serious or at least I hoped it wasn't.

My first visit to the hospital to see my friend was shocking to say the least. It was several days after the accident and I did not expect to see my friend in a coma. I did not expect to see him missing teeth and cuts allover his body. In fact, he did not look like my friend. He looked very different. He was hooked up to machines and had fluids running into his veins. I was left speechless. It almost felt as if somebody punched me in the gut and all the air was knocked out of me. Nobody was in the room to explain anything. There was only my friend dying and myself in that hospital room. After taken it all in, I stepped into the hallway. My back was against a wall and I stared straight ahead. The mother of whom was lying nearly dead feet away in the intensive care unit, stepped off the elevator nearby. She saw me with my back against the wall. She quickly walked over to me and we hugged.

She repeated, *it doesn't look good.* She kept repeating this several times and I didn't have much to say because I agreed, but couldn't say that I did. At this point, I did not know if my friend was going to get out of this thing alive. Even if he did wake up, would he be the same or less? Would he be able to walk, move, or even think? Would he remember who anyone was or how to do the simple things? At this point, nobody knew much because there were too many variables at play. The chances of him surviving and being perfectly normal were slim. This continued to cross my mind for the next several weeks.

I learned, the night of the accident my friend was drinking at another friend's house. It was obvious to many he drank too much, so they hid his keys so he could not drive home. At some point, my friend ended up finding his keys and did end up driving that night. Everyone in the house was sleeping and did not know my friend left. My friend was cruising at high speeds down the road back to his house. He did not wear his seatbelt and ended up crashing into a telephone pole at speeds of 90 mph or more. He flew out the side of the car and crushed his teeth on the asphalt. It was very early in the morning. The first responders called a helicopter to fly my friend to the nearest hospital. Fortunately, the hospital ended up saving his life.

My friend is very tough and has always been. If this accident happened to most other people, they would have certainly not made it. My friend has been known for fighting people and usually always won. In high school, he was riding his ATV down the road and ended up in a head on collision with a car. He was thrown from his ATV and ended up flying through the car's windshield. Most people that ended up flying headfirst through a windshield would take a few minutes to get situated. My friend immediately jumped back on his ATV and drove home, which was obviously illegal. The police did end up finding him. The stories about him go on and on. He was truly a tough guy, which is why I believe he survived the car crash.

I ended up visiting him every weekend on my way home from college. Most of the time, he was not awake, and we did not have any conversation. He was induced in a coma for about 1 month after the accident. They said it would have been too painful to bring him out too early. I often did see his family and would talk with them. It was very depressing and made me realize many things in life. This made me realize that we do not live forever and need to enjoy our lives while we are able to. It was evident that my friend's life would change forever because of this accident. There was no going back.

Not to get too deep into the details, but he did have a tracheostomy tube or trach tube for short. This was put in the night of the accident during the procedure to save his life. Since my friend was dying, the doctors had to act quick and get this trach tube in as quickly as possible. They may have botched the job slightly because my friend ended up needing to undergo over 50 surgeries to fix it. He was often spewing blood and mucus out of this trach hole whenever I would visit. I am still grossed out from the thought of it. This was just another reason I'd never want to end up in this situation.

When he finally did wake from the coma, he was loopy because of all the drugs. He would sit there and write on a dry-erase board nonsense. In his head, it must have made sense, but I had no clue what he was trying to communicate. It almost felt like he was a toddler and could not properly form sentences. At one point he wrote 'poop' on the dry-erase board with an arrow pointing toward it. I am still not sure till this day what that meant. As weeks went by, he became less loopy and his communication improved. He still needed to go through

much physical therapy to walk again. Since he spent
months in bed, his muscles deteriorated, and he became
very weak. This was a completely different guy from who I
knew just a few months prior.

My friend went from being a strong healthy guy to being
weak and helpless. One night created chaos for my friend,
which would last for several years. Although he realizes
today, he was wrong and should have never gotten behind
the wheel intoxicated, it simply is too late. This is
something he will never be able to take back. The years
wasted in hospitals, getting medical procedures done,
going to the dentist to get new teeth, and all the money
spent, will never be given back. I try to remember this
anytime I am about to do something 'stupid' or
'immature'. If I am working at the machine shop with my
father and I am thinking about trying something unsafe
that could save a few minutes, I think about the risks of an
accident. If I end up hurting myself, it could be an injury I
will wish I never had. It's always better to be safe than
sorry.

First of all, we are not immortal and do have a shelf-life.
We need to be grateful for our friends and family. We
need to cherish them while they are still here because
nobody lives forever. Secondly, it is crucial to learn from
others' experiences. Due to the severity and impact my
friend's near-death experience left on me, I would never
drink and drive. I would never want this for myself or
anyone else. It is incredible to see the impact it leaves on
everyone who knows that individual. Even if you did not
like my friend, you would still feel bad for him. It would
also be mentally draining for my friend. I could imagine

him laying months in his hospital bed coming to the realization that he nearly died. This would be horrible.

Although I do not like thinking about these types of events, it reminds me to make good decisions in life. My wife works for the same hospital that saved my friends life. She often comes home and tells me upsetting stories about how patients ended up in the hospital. Sometimes the treatments themselves can be just as bad as the accidents. Most upsetting are the stories about children because they are so innocent. I've realized a lot does change when you have your own children. My perspective on life has completely changed. Things that were once important to me are no longer important. Things that were not important to me are now important.

A few months after having my first child, I was on the treadmill at my gym. I saw on the news a story about a bus accident in Saskatchewan, Canada where several kids were killed. These kids all played on the same hockey team. I felt a sense of overbearing emotion come over me but did not know why. Previously, when I did not have a child, I would have not put too much thought into this sad story. Now, I do have a child and I feel I can relate. I realized these kids have parents who care about them, just like I care for my children. I would never want my own children to be harmed. I would do anything and everything possible to prevent them from being harmed.

All of this further solidifies my belief that you need to plan for the future. Unexpected events can occur at any point in your life, which is why it is extremely important to prepare sooner rather than later. You do not want to end up losing control of your life because you did not take the time to prepare. You also want to make sure you make good decisions throughout your life to reduce the risk of ending up between a rock and a hard place. As I mentioned before, I did not set myself up for success in high school. This is why I needed to work twice as hard in college to catch up. Obviously, this is not the greatest method for achieving success in any circumstance. My lack of effort in high school increased my risk of performing poorly later on in my college career.

Fortunately, by the time I completed high school and college, and started my career as a chemist, I was mature enough to know I needed to manage my money well. For starters, as a chemist my salary was low because the startup pharmaceutical company I worked for was cheap. I'm not sure if there is any better way of saying it. Unlike many of my friends who had better job offers out of college, I remained living at home. I've always gotten along well with my parents and my job was somewhat local. Instead of paying about $1,000 per month for rent, I could use this money to pay off my student loans quickly. I did not want to keep my 7-9% interest student loans around too long because I'd end up paying significant interest to the bank. I would prioritize paying off those debts as fast as possible.

It took me roughly 4 years to get rid of all my student loans. To clarify, my parents paid for the bulk of my schooling and I was left with $26,021.24. I ended up paying $3,866.24 in interest, but this could have been a lot worse if I did not expedite the debt removal process. Basically, I'd add extra principle to each payment until it was paid off. The loan was unavoidable because I needed money to go to college and I did not have this type of money just laying around. On the other hand, I purchased a new Jeep Wrangler Unlimited Sahara in 2011. This purchase was completely avoidable because I had a perfectly working 2003 Volkswagen GTI paid off. The price tag on the Jeep was $35,000, yet it ended up costing me $46,000 after interest, tags, fees, and so on. The payment for the Jeep was $569.62 per month.

When we really think about purchasing a car, boat, furniture, or any other big-ticket item, we really need to prove to ourselves that it makes sense. A lot of the time, we convince ourselves we need the item through reasoning, yet no proof is there that shows we actually need the item. We go to great lengths to convince ourselves that a big-ticket item makes sense. In the case of my Jeep, I convinced myself I would probably need a new clutch for my Volkswagen GTI soon because I felt it going. A new clutch was $2,000 or so. In reality, even if I did need a new clutch, that was less than the cost of 4 payments on the new Jeep. My GTI even had much better gas mileage in comparison to the Jeep. I also envisioned myself driving through deep puddles, climbing mountains, and blasting through snow in the Jeep. These scenarios are somewhat unlikely in New Jersey to the extent of what I imagined. I kept telling myself I work hard and deserve a new Jeep. Then without even realizing it, I am at the dealership haggling and then signing for the Jeep. Then driving off the lot, down the road 10 miles, and then it hits me. Damn it! I did not get a great deal. At this point it is too late and I now have to live with my decision.

The largest loan I've ever taken out so far in my life was my mortgage for my home. My wife and I purchased our home in 2014 in Hammonton, New Jersey, which is the blueberry capital of the World. While living with my parents, I'd run several days a week, 3 to 5 miles per day. It was during a time when I wanted to purchase a home. Instead of just driving through neighborhoods to search for houses, I felt it would be more intimate to jog through the neighborhoods. There is a difference between driving through a neighborhood in an enclosed car and actually running through the neighborhood exposed to the elements. Each time I went out for my run, I'd find a new route to take because I wanted to explore new territories. Possible areas I could live one day. At one point, I would only run around a few small streets near Hammonton Lake. It was there that I saw a few houses I liked.

There was one house that was slightly above my price range for that time in my life, but I absolutely loved it. I'd run by this house several times a week. It was motivating to me to think one day I could have a house that nice if I continued working hard. At the time the house was about 1.5 miles from my parent's place. I noticed my pace was somewhat quick until I got to the house. As I approached the house, I slowed down to get a better glimpse of it. Once I passed it, I would speed back up again until I got back home. I would daydream during the remainder of my run about living in that house. I could see myself in there with my wife and future children. I would also even think about pets and having barbecues with our future neighbors. Everything would be so fulfilling and joyous. Except, the house was listed well above my price range. This was a bit of a bubble bursting moment when I remembered, I wasn't made of cash.

During these runs to find a home, I was working as a packaging engineer for a fortune 500 company. I left the pharma startup company because my salary was too low, benefits were not great, and working conditions were poor. Additionally, I had extra income from the machine shop my father and I owned. My fiancé also had a job as an X-ray tech. Combined we were doing pretty well, but I was not confident we could afford the house near the lake because it was outside our price range. A few weeks went by from the first time I saw that house and still nobody purchased it. A few months went by and still nobody purchased it. The price was dropping dramatically because the owners wanted to sell it. The owners were divorced and had already moved out at least 1-year prior.

My wife and I decided to call our realtor to schedule a tour of this home I've ran by countless times. Upon entering the home for the first time, I knew it was the place I'd raise my family. It definitely had a unique style, which could be why others were not interested. It is not a cookie cutter house. It has a more custom feel to it. There are two sinks in the kitchen and one of those is a Talavera sink, which was imported from Mexico. The bar has cabinet doors that were hand painted with beautiful bottles of wine and grapes. There is a bathroom on the main floor with a bird theme. There is another bathroom on the main floor with a classic Italian theme containing a jacuzzi, chandelier, and fancy tiles. I will admit this bathroom is pretty loud. The basement was completely finished. The garage was very large. The living room has 18' ceilings and was also very spacious. For me this was an easy decision, especially as the price dropped.

My fiancé and I purchased the house and made it our home. Immediately after, on the day of signing for the house, I had to present to the VP of R&D at my job, and then hop on an airplane to Detroit, Michigan for work. My fiancé and her favorite cousin cleaned the house. When I returned, I finished moving my stuff from my parent's house to my new house. My fiancé, our cat, and I quickly settled into our new home. We were very cognizant of our financial situation and knew it would be tight for a few years. We would plan to pay cash for everything to avoid getting into trouble with debt. We agreed that we would discuss our expenses often and make sure we were aligned on every purchase. We were in no position to make mistakes.

We went a few weeks without furniture in our living room. It also took a few weeks for a TV. We avoided getting into trouble by purchasing items through credit cards because we knew this would be a mistake. We were smart about each purchase for the home and made sure we both agreed on every purchase as planned. The important thing was we had a home we could live in together. Everything else would fall into place when cash was available. We would also need to save for our wedding the following year, which was not going to be cheap.

After down payment, the mortgage would be $267,000. At the end of the day after paying everything off, I would have paid $451,991 over 30 years and $184,991 of that would be just for interest. When I look at that, I am thinking I could almost purchase another house for the interest I am paying to the bank. My original interest rate was 3.875%, which is actually not too bad. As I've done with my student loans, I wanted to pay off the mortgage much faster than the 30-year period because then I'd save money. Based on early calculations, I could end up saving $80,000 to $120,000 in interest, if I paid the mortgage off early. This in itself, was enough motivation to start planning out my next 10-15 years of mortgage payments.

Before I made the decision to pay my mortgage off early, I did need to consider another option. The alternative option would be to invest the extra money instead of using it to pay my mortgage off early. Let's look at a few scenarios.

Scenario 1 – Mortgage (non-accelerated plan)
Amount Borrowed = $267,000
Period of payment = 360 months or 30 years
Mortgage interest rate = 3.875%
Extra principal payment per month = $0

First year of amortization (non-accelerated plan)

month	beginning	pmt	interest	principal	ending balance
january	$267,000.00	$1,255.53	$862.19	$393.35	$266,606.65
february	$266,606.65	$1,255.53	$860.92	$394.62	$266,212.04
march	$266,212.04	$1,255.53	$859.64	$395.89	$265,816.15
april	$265,816.15	$1,255.53	$858.36	$397.17	$265,418.98
may	$265,418.98	$1,255.53	$857.08	$398.45	$265,020.53
june	$265,020.53	$1,255.53	$855.80	$399.74	$264,620.79
july	$264,620.79	$1,255.53	$854.50	$401.03	$264,219.76
august	$264,219.76	$1,255.53	$853.21	$402.32	$263,817.44
september	$263,817.44	$1,255.53	$851.91	$403.62	$263,413.82
october	$263,413.82	$1,255.53	$850.61	$404.93	$263,008.89
november	$263,008.89	$1,255.53	$849.30	$406.23	$262,602.66
december	$262,602.66	$1,255.53	$847.99	$407.55	$262,195.11

Scenario 1 speaks to normal mortgage payments with no additional payment towards principal and no investments. The loan would be paid off in 30 years. The interest paid

over the 30 years would be $184,991. This is what the banks would want you to do because it maximizes the money they earn from you in the form of interest.

Scenario 2 – Mortgage (accelerated plan)
Amount Borrowed = $267,000
Period of payment = 150 months or 12.5 years
Mortgage interest rate = 3.875%
Extra principal payment per month = $1,000

First year of amortization (accelerated plan)

month	beginning	pmt	interest	principal	ending balance
january	$267,000.00	$2,255.53	$862.19	$1,393.35	$265,606.65
february	$265,606.65	$2,255.53	$857.69	$1,397.84	$264,208.81
march	$264,208.81	$2,255.53	$853.17	$1,402.36	$262,806.45
april	$262,806.45	$2,255.53	$848.65	$1,406.89	$261,399.56
may	$261,399.56	$2,255.53	$844.10	$1,411.43	$259,988.13
june	$259,988.13	$2,255.53	$839.55	$1,415.99	$258,572.15
july	$258,572.15	$2,255.53	$834.97	$1,420.56	$257,151.58
august	$257,151.58	$2,255.53	$830.39	$1,425.15	$255,726.44
september	$255,726.44	$2,255.53	$825.78	$1,429.75	$254,296.69
october	$254,296.69	$2,255.53	$821.17	$1,434.37	$252,862.32
november	$252,862.32	$2,255.53	$816.53	$1,439.00	$251,423.32
december	$251,423.32	$2,255.53	$811.89	$1,443.65	$249,979.68

Scenario 2 speaks to accelerated mortgage payments. This scenario has $1,000 extra going to principal each month and will allow you to pay off the mortgage early. An extra $1,000 per month on this mortgage will get the debt removed in 12.5 years. Once the mortgage is paid off after 12.5 years, I would then invest the $1,255 mortgage payment plus $1,000 extra principal per month. At 7.5%

ROI, I'd expect to gain $491,000 or more after 17 years. I use 17 years because that would take us to the 30-year mark and we can compare against the other two scenarios.

Scenario 3 – Investment route

Investment interest rate = 7.5%
Yearly amount invested = $12,000
Period of investment = 360 months of 30 years

Investment route

year	start	end	year	start	end
1	$12,000.00	$12,931.59	16	$356,717.35	$384,410.24
2	$24,931.59	$26,867.10	17	$396,410.24	$427,184.60
3	$38,867.10	$41,884.45	18	$439,184.60	$473,279.64
4	$53,884.45	$58,067.64	19	$485,279.64	$522,953.16
5	$70,067.64	$75,507.17	20	$534,953.16	$576,482.97
6	$87,507.17	$94,300.58	21	$588,482.97	$634,168.43
7	$106,300.58	$114,552.97	22	$646,168.43	$696,332.17
8	$126,552.97	$136,377.61	23	$708,332.17	$763,321.83
9	$148,377.61	$159,896.55	24	$775,321.83	$835,512.08
10	$171,896.55	$185,241.32	25	$847,512.08	$913,306.65
11	$197,241.32	$212,553.68	26	$925,306.65	$997,140.61
12	$224,553.68	$241,986.36	27	$1,009,140.61	$1,087,482.81
13	$253,986.36	$273,703.99	28	$1,099,482.81	$1,184,838.52
14	$285,703.99	$307,883.93	29	$1,196,838.52	$1,289,752.21
15	$319,883.93	$344,717.35	30	$1,301,752.21	$1,402,810.61

Scenario 3 speaks to using the extra $1,000 per month on an investment with a ROI (return on investment) of 7.5%. This would also include you paying off your mortgage with no extra payments as shown in scenario 1. This is typically what most financial advisors would recommend, but I've always been skeptical due to risk.

I have created a table laying out each scenario to compare starting amounts, interest, and results. As most financial advisors would suggest, the favorable scenario based on numbers is the investment route. Although, this is most favorable in terms of numbers, there are associated risks in investing versus using your money to pay down debts first. There is always the risk of not getting a favorable ROI. At that point, you would have nothing to show for your hard-earned money that you invested. You will also need to think about fees your financial advisor or stock broker charge for their services. Lastly, you will need to retain a large debt for the full length of the loan. In this case it is 30-years and that is pretty long.

Investment versus mortgage payoff summary

Scenario	Starting amount	Interest	End point
SCENARIO 1 Non-accelerated mortgage	$267,000 debt	$184,991 paid for mortgage $0 gained from investment	$0 debt in 30 years
SCENARIO 2 Accelerated mortgage	$267,000 debt	$69,990 paid for mortgage $491,006 gained from investment over 17 years after mortgage paid off	$0 debt in 12.5 year $491K plus earned in interest in 30 years
SCENARIO 3 Investment route	$267,000 debt	$184,991 paid for mortgage $1,042,810 gained from investment over 30 years	$0 debt in 30 years $1 million plus earned in interest in 30 years

When you subtract the mortgage interest from investment interest gained in scenario 3, you end up with $857,819. When you subtract the mortgage interest from the investment interest gained in scenario 2, you end up with $349,016. By selecting scenario 2 (accelerated mortgage) instead of scenario 3 (investment route), you are theoretically losing $508,803.

Of course, the decision is up to you because you will need to live with it. Based on risk and my skepticism for the current stock market, I decided to first payoff my mortgage. I do contribute to my 401(k), especially because my employer matches up to 4% of my salary. The majority of employer's match between 0 to 6%, so at 4% I feel pretty good. Although they only match 4%, I contribute much higher at 15% of my annual salary. I feel good at this level of contribution because they say you should save at least 10% of your salary. If all else fails, I will have the 15% of my salary contribution + 4% employer match in my 401(k).

Another reason I prioritized paying off my mortgage over heavy investing is for peace of mind. Once I remove my mortgage, I will feel more stable and less worried about losing my job. If I ended up losing my job while having a mortgage payment, then I'd feel extremely worried about how I'd make those payments. Without a mortgage payment, I could quickly get a half decent job and be 'okay' for a while. Some may agree, while others disagree. At the end of the day it is personal preference. How much risk are you willing to take?

In life we can never really be 100% certain that we are going to be in the same situation or better year over year.

Unexpected events can present themselves and it is our job to manage those events the best we can. For my friend who nearly ended up dead because of the car accident, he never really ended up finishing school or starting a career. It has been 12 years since the accident and he still lives at his parent's house. As the years go on, it becomes more challenging for my friend to justify finishing school or getting a job. He feels as if he has fallen into a hole and cannot get out.

Then there are the people who lost it all, yet they never stop trying and are triumphant several years later. Sadly, I do not think this will happen to my friend. He simply is not that type of person. He also would not take advice off others because he is stubborn. We need to keep in mind, we cannot change everyone. Those who are stubborn are going to be stubborn with or without you. Our biggest priority is making sure we are getting what we need. If there is someone you know that is stubborn and does not take advice, it is sometimes best to let him or her go. You can only push so hard before something breaks. Efforts will be better spent on your own initiatives. The stubborn people will need to wake up on their own and want to change things around.

The world is constantly changing around us, and we need to continue learning new things every day. Even if we find ourselves falling behind, it may not be too late to catch up and eventually advance ahead of others. During my high school career, I would say I was very behind the pack. During my college career, I had to put in significant effort to stay side by side with the pack, but I felt I was just barely making it. Again, as a chemist I was building momentum, but was certainly not ahead of the pack.

Then as I transitioned into other roles such as maintenance, packaging, and eventually in supply chain, I could feel a big shift. This shift felt good because I could see my efforts were paying off.

I've always considered myself the hare in the story, *the tortoise and the hare.* My focus is on small gains over an extended period of time and rarely the type to sprint passed others in a race. My strengths are my stamina, patience, and persistence. Overtime, I have gained momentum to pull ahead of the other competitors in the race. In high school, I do not think anyone thought of me as most likely to succeed. As time went by, I started to see more believers who felt I could actually succeed in something. They may not have necessarily knew what my success would be, but they knew it would happen. Today, I have proven results and people believe in me. Most importantly, my family and I believe in me. The part about *me, believing in me,* took me a good amount of time.

A key ingredient to our success is having the ***ability to learn***. Learning does not stop once you finish with school. Learning continues throughout life and it is up to you to take learning opportunities seriously. When others go through challenging times in their life, you should really appreciate their suffering and learn from their mistakes. When others have been successful, congratulate them and take some key learnings from these events too. Our experiences also factor into our continued growth and should also be taken seriously. If you prevent yourself from learning, then you are preventing yourself from being successful.

From my friend's accident in 2007, I learned a lot and would be remiss if I did not mention this. We don't need to be in the car crash to realize this was an incredibly tragic event. Similarly, you don't need to jump off a cliff to know it is not smart. As people, we are smart enough to realize when things are moronic. This is why we should not only learn from other's successes, but other's failures too. Sharing information between friends and family is a good idea to enable advancement. At the time, my friend did have family members who ended up crashing in cars or getting pulled over by police while under the influence of alcohol. This may have been something he should have already knew not to do or perhaps, he felt this was just standard living.

We will also need to keep our eyes open for standard practices that we are accustomed to, which need to be changed. If my friend's family traditionally drove cars under the influence, then my friend may have not realized it was wrong. Normal behaviors are defined by your surroundings. In addition to learning from other's mistakes, we need to question the so called 'normal behaviors' occurring every day. This is important to our survival and progression towards success.

Anytime I think about *baby steps*, I think about the 1991 movie titled *What About Bob?* Bill Murray played Bob Wiley who was a patient of Dr. Leo Marvin, who was played by Richard Dreyfuss. This movie is simply a classic and I must have watched it at least 50 times. It was a family favorite whenever my grandpa and uncle would come visit us. In the movie Dr. Marvin wrote a book called, *Baby Steps*. The concept was all about taking things slow and baby stepping your way out of your problems. There is a reason I am talking about this and not just to purely reminisce.

Over the years, I've grasped onto a concept I call, **small gains**. Small gains are consistent baby steps forward that can be added up over an extended period of time, to give you a large gain. As we know great things rarely ever happen overnight. Usually great things involve planning and executing the plan over a lengthy period of time. This is partly why many do not reach success. Lack of patience. Everybody wants everything today or they simply just give up. I can assure you this is not the correct approach to getting what you want. I have a better way.

Think about all the knowledge you have today. Most likely you gained the knowledge from various parts of your life. In the early stages of life, we are learning how to crawl, walk, talk, and so on. Later in life, we start going to school and learning how to do arts and crafts. We are starting to socialize with other kids and learning how to share. Then we get into basic math, science, geography, music, and grammar courses. As we progress forward, we are learning more challenging materials. Eventually, we are juniors and seniors in high school, planning for our futures once we leave high school. Some of us attend college, while others immediately join the workforce or go into the military.

Whatever the path, we are all learning and storing this knowledge in our brain for future use. At some point, you may realize you are more interested in a certain area and those materials will be more important to you. For example, as a chemist I was most interested in chemistry topics. Any chemistry topic would be something I would put my focus on. For 3 years as a chemist, the majority of my focus was on chemistry and learning how I could leverage this knowledge to do my job better. When we are interested in a topic or it is connected to something we are currently doing, the information is more meaningful. This information will more readily absorb into our brains and stay there for longer than meaningless materials.

I consider each newly learned material a building block. The expectation is to create something larger from the several building blocks you picked up along the way. My prerequisite to be a chemist was my degree in biochemistry. In college, I needed to fulfill all requirements for the degree. To succeed, I needed to make sure I understood all materials and earned passing grades on my exams and assignments. Elementary school, junior high school, and high school were all necessary to get into college. These earlier years helped me get the building blocks I needed to succeed. It is easy to look back to see where I came from. It is not always easy to look forward and determine where I am going.

In order to be successful, we need to make sure we set clear goals and expectations. I have included here a portion of a *5-year tracker* I created in Microsoft excel to build my plans for the next 5-years. This is just one way of doing it. There are many other ways to plan and track your goals. Keep in mind, I am only showing two years of the table and the goals are just examples. I did not include actual dollar amounts.

It is important to layout the various areas of your life that you want to focus on. For example, I have listed my career, education, personal business, and personal life. The last row titled, accomplishments (end of year review) is where you'd write down the results of what you actually accomplished. This is a very important step. As always, we want to make sure we are recognizing our results.

5-year tracker

	Year 1	Year 2
	2019	2020
	Age - 29	Age - 30
Career	Salary $ XX Bonus $ XX	Salary $ XX (increase 3%) Bonus $ XX (increase 3%)
Education	Start masters program	Complete 12 credit hours
Personal Business	Gross sales $ XX Profitability $ XX	Gross sales $ XX (increase 5%) Profitability $ XX (increase 5%)
Personal Life	Payoff 25% of mortgage 401(k) $ XX Get married	Payoff 40% of mortgage 401(k) $ XX (increase 7%) Have a baby Visit Germany
Accomplishments (End of Year Review)		

It is also important to layout a timeline across the top row. I like to note my age as an extra frame of reference. The challenging, yet fun part is to create your goals and expectations for each year. In the career row, I usually stick to my salary and bonus. You can also speak to your level, role, and any promotion you are working towards. You could also go into the detail of plans to transition from company to company, department to department, role to role, and so on. We are not worried about how we are going to get there when filling out the 5-year tracker. However, the goals should be realistic.

The education part is always important to me. This bucket speaks to continued education, which is crucial to career growth. It is not just receiving a piece of paper that says you have completed a degree in whatever you studied. It is the knowledge you gained from the schooling and lessons learned. As much as people do not want to admit it, the name of your school also carries some weight. The people you meet during school also play a role in your future success. Networking can lead to opportunities, which is why we need to be our best every day. You never know who can help you reach that next level.

Not everyone has a personal business. This may or may not be applicable to you. I speak to gross sales and profitability because those are important to me. You could also speak to future plans of expanding your business. You could talk about new innovations or patents you would like to obtain. You could even speak to the number of employees you'd like to employ in the next 5-years. If you have 1 employee today, you may want 5 employees in two years. These are good details to flesh out in your 5-year plan tracker.

In the personal bucket, I've listed out a goal to pay off my mortgage. I also wrote goals around increasing my 401(k), getting married, and having a baby. As all of these buckets are personal, the goals you write are going to be what you deem as important. The point of this exercise is to show you a way to track your goals year over year. To clarify, I've already gotten married and had a baby. These are just examples someone may write. You will want to document the goal description and timing. You will want to record the results at the bottom of the table, so you can reflect on your performance. Higher or lower than expected performance may influence you to raise or lower your targets for the next few years.

The plan to reach the goal will not be documented in this 5-year tracker. I would typically keep the detailed plan in a separate notebook because there would not be enough space in the 5-year tracker. The 5-year plan tracker is a high-level overview of all your goals in an easy to read form. In a separate notebook or electronic document, you would write the goal, timing, and plan to achieve that goal. You may also want to track the detailed progress in the notebook. I keep a journal where I track my daily thoughts and progress towards goals. This keeps me engaged and prevents me from forgetting goals. If you write your goals in a notebook that you review frequently, then that method works too. It is important you select a method that works for you. You will be the one using it, so it doesn't matter that other people prefer a different method. Your preferred method will work best for you.

When we are setting goals, we will want to make them reasonable and not too outrageous. On the other side of the spectrum, we will not want to make them too easy. There are people who purposely set goals too high. When they do not succeed, they feel as if it is justifiable based on the difficulty of what they set out to achieve. There are people who set goals too low and will never fail. We want to set our goals in the upper-middle portion in terms of difficulty. We should be stretching slightly to reach our goals, but not too much where we would get burned out and quit.

If we think about goal setting, we are going to have various goals in different areas of difficulty. If we take the example of paying off a mortgage. The easy range may be paying off 5% of the mortgage per year. So, 5% of a $200,000 mortgage would require you to pay off $10,000 per year. The hard range may require you to pay off 20% per year or $40,000. You would want to focus on the higher mid-range. So, you would write into your 5-year plan table under personal goals, *payoff 12.5% of mortgage* in the first year. In the second year, *payoff 25% of mortgage*. In the third year, *payoff 37.5% of mortgage*. As we can see we are making gains each year to achieve the final goal, which would be *payoff 100% of mortgage*. At this rate of 12.5% each year, it would take us 8 years to achieve this goal.

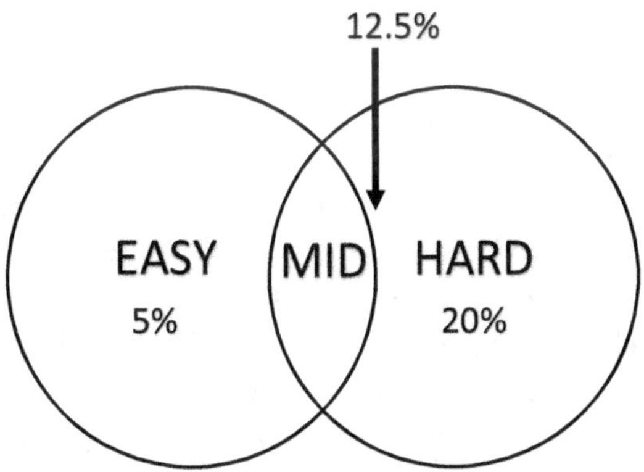

Everyone's situation is a little bit different and I am just using examples here. The overlapping circles illustrated can be used in many situations. It is up to you to create a goal and determine the upper and lower difficulty range. Then you'd determine where the middle is and target a little bit higher than that. The other thing you'd want to think about is the return on investment. We do not simply chase difficult goals for the sake of challenging ourselves. We need to receive some sort of benefit from our hard work.

Imagine there is an open role in your company. The role is more challenging than your current role and the pay is actually less. Chances are, you are not going to apply for the open role because you do not want to make less money for a job that is more difficult. We can relate this to our goals. If you setup a goal that is challenging and there is not much benefit there, then why would you take on this challenge? A good example of this is earning a graduate degree that will not provide you any benefit going forward. If you are an accountant, then why would you get a graduate degree in botany, especially knowing you will never need it? Unless you are very passionate about plants, I'd recommend against earning a degree that will not benefit you.

We can also speak to undergraduate degrees and how so many have wasted years of their life earning a degree that did not get them their dream job. There is an astounding amount of college graduates that do not work in a field that matches up with what they studied in college. According to an article by Annie Nova on CNBC.com titled, *Why your first job out of college really, really matters,* more than 40 percent of college graduates take positions out of school that don't require a degree. 1 in 5 college grads still aren't working a degree-demanding job a decade after leaving school. Three-quarters of these graduates who took jobs early on that didn't demand a degree will be in the same spot and these graduates earn around $10,000 a year less than their counterparts who started early in jobs that required a college degree.

When we think about $10,000 less per year, we may not think it is a huge deal. Over 10-years, that would be $100,000 and this is the way we should be thinking about a lot of things. When you go into a car dealership and they ask you how much you want to pay per month, they are trying to get you to think about the short-term versus the long-term. A car salesman will say it is only $500 per month, but over 60 months that is $30,000. What is the original cost of the vehicle? The car may actually only be $20,000, so you are paying $10,000 too much. We need to think long-term and what the total cost is to our pockets. Whether it is a lower salary, higher car payment, or higher utility bill each month, we need to challenge it. The car dealership, utility companies, and our employers want us to be satisfied with paying a little more and getting a little less. They want us to think it is not a big deal, but overtime it becomes a big deal.

When we create our future plans in the 5-year tracker, we are laying out goals. These goals will remind us daily that we are working towards something. Each day counts, which is why we need to make sure we are moving forward each day. If we let our utility company charge us an extra $5 per month, it equates to $60 extra dollars per year. Over 10-years, that is an extra $600 on top of our normal bill. In 10-years, our utility company will not just

up charge us once. They will continually do this each year.
In year one, you may be paying $100 per month for a
utility. In year two, you are up to $105 per month. In the
next eight years the monthly bill is $110, $115, $120, $125,
$130, $135, $140, $145, and then $150. In year one at
$100, you are paying $6,000 per year. In year ten, at $150,
you are paying $9,000 per year. The extra $3,000 per year
will prevent us from reaching our goals. Each year, we
need to challenge the utility company to make sure they
are not hiking up the bill too much.

Another tracker I use for my time is the ***Activity Tracker***.
In life, we have limited time to accomplish everything we
want to do. In Microsoft excel I created a table to layout
my activities, time spent for each of those activities, and
the benefit of each activity. This helps us understand what
activities are consuming most of our time. It also helps us
prioritize what is essential and what is not. On my activity
tracker I've listed health, personal business, career (+
commute), family, and sleep. These are the essential
activities in my life. These are the activities I prioritize.

Each of these activities has a benefit listed to justify why I
am spending the time on that activity. For example, the
gym's benefit is healthy body. To live a quality life, I feel it
is necessary to keep my body healthy. This activity takes
6% or 10 hours per week, so I think it makes sense. My
personal business is to generate extra money and only
takes 5% per week. In reality, this should be much higher,
but this activity tracker was a snapshot from a time in my
life when my personal business activity was low. The
important part of this is to learn how to apply this table to
your own life activities.

The career (+commute) is my primary salary and takes 36% of my time per week. To clarify, there are 168 hours per week (7 days per week x 24 hours per day = 168 hours per week). I've added family at 21% and sleep at 25% of my weekly time. At the end of the day, I have 8% of my time free for other activities. I would strongly recommend you going through a similar exercise with your own activities. You may be surprised with how much time you are spending in non-essential activities that can and should be removed. An activity is deemed essential if it provides you a benefit that would be considered necessary.

Activity Tracker

ACTIVITY	DAYS PER WEEK	HOURS PER DAY	TIME SPENT (HR)	%TIME/WK (168 HR)	Benefit(s)
Gym	5	2	10	6%	healthy body
Personal Business	4	2	8	5%	extra money
Career (+ Commute)	5	12	60	36%	salary
Family	7	5	35	21%	emotional support
Sleep	7	6	42	25%	re-energize
Total			155	92%	
Leftover			13	8%	

I must emphasize non-essential activities need to be removed from your schedule. When we are spread too thin or have too many items to focus on, we tend to work really hard and not go anywhere. The old saying, *I've got my wheels turning, but I'm not going anywhere* does apply here. Non-essential activities that add no significant benefit to the overall picture will only take up more time and give you more stress. I have learned this the hard way and because I've been working on non-essential activities for so long, it was really hard to forget about them. One example of this was my blog, which did not provide me with a ton of benefit, but was consuming more of my time.

I have also learned that working on non-essential activities for too long makes them feel as if they are essential. I have a bit of OCD (obsessive-compulsive disorder) where I feel I need to go through each step of a process, even if the steps are non-value add. If I am cutting my lawn, I will typically finish by using a weed whacker and blow off my driveway with a blower. Even if the weed whacker or blower were not necessary, I feel I still need to use them to complete the task. In life, there are sometimes steps we can skip over from time to time. It is up to us to make the decision. In recent years, I've done a much better job of determining when steps can be skipped. This has helped me save time and be more effective. As a disclaimer, do not skip critical steps that are crucial to success.

When I think about the activity-time tracker, I try to relate each of these activities to my 5-year plan tracker, where I am recording all my goals. I ask myself, how does the gym provide me with results for my goals over the next five years? How does my career provide me with results for my goals over the next five years? Am I using my time appropriately to make sure I achieve my goals? What is important to me? I often ask myself challenging questions to make sure I am making the right decisions. I'd rather ask myself the tough questions than have someone else ask me those questions and not have an answer.

As I mentioned earlier, learning is part of a building block experience to create the mass of knowledge you have today. Similarly, yearly goals are the building blocks to create your overall 5-year plan or 10-year plan goals. In the 5-year plan goal tracker, I listed 4 focus areas. These were health, personal business, education, and career. Each of these can be viewed as a pillar to the overarching goal, *early retirement*.

Pillars to success

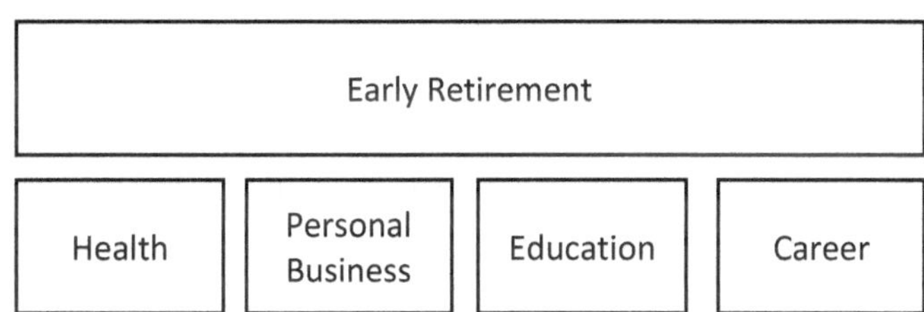

Each of these 4 focus areas have specific goals I need to reach each year. From year to year, the goals do not seem significant. It is when you look at the overall progress from year one to year five, that is when you see significant progress. Without each of the 4 pillars, the overarching goal of early retirement is not possible.

As important as it is to ask questions, it is equally important to gain answers. I realized as I progressed forward in my career, I went from not knowing what questions to ask, to asking the questions, and finally to knowing the answers. There is a time and place for everything. As I progress forward, I see myself making more statements and becoming more of an authority on certain topics. An example of this is in the field of packaging. By no means, am I the most knowledgeable packaging engineer that ever lived, but I can get the answers to my questions pretty quickly. I can also influence others cross-functionally to proceed with my recommendations. These are important skills to have, but not always easy to obtain.

In high school and college, it is very rare to be taught how to properly write a business professional e-mail. I could see the confusion and lack of confidence when managing interns during my time in packaging. This simple task was very new to them and new to me at one time. Business meeting educate can also be intimidating when you are new. When can I speak? Who can I speak to? How do I speak to them? These are questions I would often hear from my interns. These were questions I once had when I first joined the business environment.

At one point when I first joined the fortune 500 company, I setup a meeting to discuss a project I was working on. There were some unanswered questions that we needed the team to discuss. I sent out the meeting invite to about 5 or 6 people from various groups in R&D. On the day of the meeting, I walked down to the room with my manager. Others quickly shuffled in behind me and the door closed behind the last one to enter the room. We all sat around the table in silence. Everyone looked at me, including my manager. My manager immediately knew I had no clue what the hell I was doing. She spoke up and gave the background on the discussion we wanted to have. I stayed pretty quiet throughout the meeting.

Thinking back at this moment, I must have looked like a real fool. Why would I setup a meeting and not have anything to say? Today, this is all second nature to me. Today, I hold conference calls with over 20 people and have no issue giving background information and guiding the conversation. In school, I was never taught how to lead a meeting. As a chemist, I was also not taught how to hold a meeting because we typically didn't have formal meetings. If we did, my manager at the time would always lead them. I was always interested in leading meetings and improving my business acumen but was never given the opportunity as a chemist.

Within the first year at the fortune 500 company, I improved my meeting educate. I also became a better presenter, but this was not easy. This took lots of practice and adjustment in my style. I did take a public speaking class in college, but I did not take it too seriously. I was more worried about what my peer students would think than actually learning the course materials. Again, this was another mistake I made in my life. I should have focused on course material and tried my best to succeed in the class. This would have helped me later in life when I was presenting as a professional.

Again, this all goes back to building blocks and making small gains to get to the next level. Another embarrassing moment I had, which ended up being beneficial was the time I setup a meeting for an entire department. This was early in my career as a packaging engineer at the fortune 500 company. There were over 90 attendees at the meeting, and I attempted to make it fun by getting everyone to play a game. When I went up to the podium and grabbed the microphone to speak, I had trouble getting control of the room. Eventually the room calmed down and I began explaining the game to everyone, but I could instantly tell the majority of the group was confused. At this point, I was a little bit confused too.

We somehow got through the game and a few folks participated to share their experience. All feedback was positive, but I knew I could have done a better job. First of all, I did not focus on my audience and focused more on the game. I was too busy thinking about the contents of this silly game I wanted everyone to play as an icebreaker. If I paid attention to who my audience was a little more, I would have realized it was not the best of ideas. My audience was science & technology. The group was made up of engineers, chemists, product developers, and technicians. It just wasn't the group to play this silly game with. I also could have been a bit more clear on explaining the game. Never again would I make this mistake.

There was another embarrassing, yet funny moment a few years later with a smaller group. I was presenting to marketing and sales some packaging updates. On a slide, I intended to have the words 'shift test'. Unfortunately, I misspelled shift and it said, 'shit test'. One of the senior brand managers said, what does that say? Everyone had a little bit of a giggle, but inside I was slightly embarrassed. From that point on, I make sure I proofread my slides thoroughly. Sometimes, I even ask others to proofread my slides prior to the meeting because I'd not want to repeat this mistake. More time upfront for preparation goes a long way.

I've learned over the years it is acceptable to say you don't know. It is bound to happen when you are presenting, and questions come at you left and right. There are bound to be questions that you simply need to follow-up on. It is better to be truthful and admit you do not know something, than flat out lie. You can always note the question and respond with an answer at a later time. I have seen others blatantly lie and I'm not afraid to call them out. I have very little patience when it comes to lies because people are making decisions based on these lies. Nothing good ever comes out of a lie.

In this chapter, we covered a lot of ground. We started by discussing the idea of small gains, which is similar to Dr. Leo Marvin's *Baby Step concept* from the movie *What about Bob?* This is a concept you will want to keep in mind as we move forward. Most great things are not built in one day. In fact, it would be a rare occurrence to create a masterpiece in one day. More often than not, great achievements take years. This is why we must push for small gains.

We are also gathering building blocks along the way and these building blocks act as our pillars to our overarching goals. My 4 areas I focus my goals on are health, personal business, education, and my career. Each of these 4 pillars or building blocks contribute in some way to my overarching goal of early retirement. Early retirement would require me to have enough funds to support this goal. My career and personal business are the cash generators to support the majority of my overarching goal. Education helps me improve what I do by gaining more knowledge and therefore, having the ability to make smart choices. Health is also an important category because I need to be physically and mentally able to perform and make money.

In this chapter, I've also discussed the topic of setting clear goals and tracking those goals. As I mentioned, this is extremely important to make sure you are making yourself accountable for your results. Refer the 5-year plan tracker as a template to track your goals, which utilizes different focus areas. Your goal setting should be appropriate in terms of difficulty and reward. It is optimal to create goals that are upper-mid difficulty range with a significant reward if successful. You should also be using the activity tracker as discussed to help you prioritize your time. Remove all non-essential activities to make sure you are effective in accomplishing the essential activities.

Being able to prioritize is another key ingredient in being successful. Without prioritization, you will not be able to function strategically and can end up wasting a lot of time on non-essential activities. Recall, essential activities have some sort of benefit to your overarching goal. You will also need to prioritize from time to time between essential activities. Basically, which essential activities must be completed now and have the biggest impact on your plan for success.

There's a lot of information here, so you may need to go back and read through again. The activity tracker and 5-year plan tracker are examples of how you can track your goals and time spent on each activity. You should modify as needed to fit your current situation. It is possible you will need to modify your trackers several times to get it just right for your needs. The important thing is you start tracking and start immediately. Waiting for the perfect day is not going to help you get to your goals any faster.

The small gains concept is briefly discussed in the previous chapter, but I would like to peel back the onion a little bit more. By now, you know I am more of a tortoise than a hare. This does not mean you need to be a tortoise. If you have enough stamina, you might be more of a hare. The concept of small gains is built around making many subtle advances over a stretch of time. When adding these subtle advances together, you will see a large advance from beginning to end. The reason many people don't push for small gains is because they feel the small gain is just that, *small*. In other words, they believe a small gain is insignificant to their overall success.

In this example below, the starting salary in 2016 is $50,000. The increase in salary each year is 3%. The Δ (change) from year to year is listed in the last row. The total change for the five years is $6,275. So, in 2020 the salary is $6,275 more than when the employee first started in 2016. Total income over 5 years with 3% salary increase each year is $265,457. The total income over 5 years with no salary increase would have been $250,000. With the 3% increase each year, you have gained an extra $15,457 in 5 years.

	2016	2017	2018	2019	2020	Total
Salary	$50,000	$51,500	$53,045	$54,636	$56,275	$265,457
Δ	0	$1,500	$1,545	$1,591	$1,639	$6,275

Now, let's look at starting expenses being $30,000 in 2016 and these expenses being reduced 3% each year. In the first year of cost reduction, $900 is saved. In the second year of cost reduction, $873 is saved. With 3% reduction year over year for 5 years, $8,734 is saved in total.

	2016	2017	2018	2019	2020	TOTAL
Expenses	$30,000	$29,100	$28,227	$27,380	$26,559	$141,266
Δ	0	($900)	($873)	($847)	($821)	($3,441)

In a 5-year period, between 3% yearly salary increases and 3% yearly expense reductions, you gain a total of $24,191. For this example, 3% is used because this typically represents yearly inflation. The push for a 3% salary increase and 3% expense reduction is on you. The majority of good companies will provide on average an annual salary increase of 3%. It does require you to be an employee who performs and gets results. A stretch goal could be 4% increase or maybe even 5%. This annual salary increase is pretty straightforward. The expense reduction is a little bit more complicated and difficult for most.

First, let's understand the basics of money management. We must understand 4 fundamental factors of money management, which include income, expense, debt, and savings.

- ***Income*** – money received, especially on a regular basis, for work or through investments
- ***Expense*** – cost required for something; the money spent on something
- ***Debt*** – money that is owed or due
- ***Savings*** – money one has saved, especially through a bank or official scheme

For simplicity, I look at income and savings as good things. I look at expense and debt as bad things. There is one more definition we should know, which is **budget** and it is defined as *an estimate of income and expenditure for a set period of time.* Here is an example of things you may consider in your budget.

Income	Expense
Salary	Utilities (e.g. electric, gas)
Earned interest	Credit cards
	Cable/internet
	Cellular phone service
	Water
	Mortgage
	Home insurance
	Auto insurance
	Property tax
	Student loans
	Food

The income is where you'd push for a >3% salary increase each year. The expense portion is where you'd push for a >3% expense reduction each year. There are many ways you can receive the reduction in expenses, but it can be challenging. It is possible to shop around for cost savings on several of the items listed such as cable, internet, cellular phone service, and insurance. You can also remove non-essential expenses altogether, which can be difficult because we might feel things like cable are essential. In reality, cable is a 'nice to have' and not a 'must have'.

As shown in the previous chapter, tracking is important to make sure you are hitting your targets. To help you setup a tracker of your own to manage your budget monthly, I included a **Monthly Financial Tracker** for your review. The top portion speaks to 'money-in'. In this example, a savings account, checking account, and 401K are listed. The bottom portion of the table speaks to 'money-out' or expenses. This includes electric, gas, credit card, cellular phone, water, mortgage, home insurance, property taxes, car loan, and student loans. By subtracting the *total debt* from *total saved*, we get *actual money* we have. You can build in assets if you want to track those in here too. Remember, this should fit your needs.

Monthly Financial Tracker

	January	February
Savings	$1,000	1,200
Checking	$1,000	1,200
401K	$5,000	5,500
Total Saved	**$7,000**	**$7,900**
Electric	$100	$100
Gas	$100	$100
Credit Card	$200	$200
Cable / Internet	$100	$100
Cellular Phone	$100	$100
Water	$25	$25
Mortgage	$1,500	$1,500
Home insurance	$200	$200
Property Taxes	$200	$200
Car loan	$350	$350

Car insurance	$100	$100
Student loans	$500	$500
Total Debt	**$3,675**	**$3,675**
Actual Money I have	**$3,325**	**$4,225**

Keep in mind, only January and February are shown. If you created a similar table in Microsoft Excel, then you would also have the other ten months listed out too. The data you are collecting here will help you set your budget going forward. When you first start, you will not have any data. The first year is then treated as a data collection year. In the second year, you should start seeing some similarities and differences from the previous year. In the third year, you are going to have some more clarity on trends from the data collected over several years. At this point, you will also gain knowledge on your financials that you did not have previously.

Here is the approach to creating an accurate budget. First, there is data collection.
- Use readily available tools given by expenditure companies (e.g. bill history and statements).
- Understand the statements and what you are purchasing.

Create a table similar to that shown in the previous page.
- Allows for quick read on financial progress.
- Generates self-awareness of income and expenses on a month to month basis.

Set goals.
- Goals should be based off of data collection.

- Shooting too high will create higher failure rates.
- Shooting too low will not allow you to grow.

For me, there is something magical about paying off debts and doing it quickly. There is a satisfaction of knowing I have a good job and have the power to free myself of that burden we call debt. I would never want to live pay check to pay check, but there are plenty of people out there that have no choice. There are single mothers working two full-time jobs just to keep food on the table. There are families living in poverty with very little hope of getting out. It is easy to say, get a job and work your way up when you have not been there. For these people who are living in poverty, there are many who are really trying with very little success.

My father did not have much as a kid, but most importantly had love from his mother and father. As a young boy living in Chatham, Ontario (Canada) he would find activities that did not cost money because quite simply, he did not have money. He lived down the street from Fergie Jenkins who became a professional baseball player for the Philadelphia Phillies, Chicago Cubs, Texas Rangers, and Boston Red Sox. Fergie was inducted into the Hall of Fame in 1991. My father also lived near Bill Atkinson who also played in the major leagues for the Montreal Expos and Chicago White Sox. Both Fergie and Bill were pitchers. Bill was not as famous as Fergie, but still made it to the big leagues. My father did not make it to the big leagues, which makes sense because he did not play baseball. He was too poor to play any organized sports.

My father told himself at an early age, he wanted better
for his children. He wanted his children to have the
opportunity to play baseball. He didn't want his children
to feel poor and not have the same opportunities as other
kids. What if my father lived on a street where there was
something in the water that made you a great pitcher? He
would never know because he didn't have the money to
play baseball. At the end of the day, he wanted much
better for his kids.

Since the age of 12 years old, my father would try making
money doing different jobs. One of his first jobs was
sweeping Jack the barber's shop between haircuts. He
would also cut lawns, paint fences, and shovel snow. At
some point he even worked as a paid pallbearer for other
people's funerals. My grandpa would take my father with
him on his route to pick up fatty tissue, bones, and other
unusable animal parts. My grandpa worked for a
rendering company that would take the unusable animal
parts and convert them into useable products. At one
point, my father said he fell into the back of the truck on
all the gross animal parts. Interestingly, my grandpa also
met James Hoffa in Michigan during one of his trips.

Years later when my father was a senior in high school, he
started working at a local food manufacturing plant. After
high school he ended up picking up another job at another
food manufacturing plant at the same time. So, he was
working two full time jobs at two different food
manufacturing plants. This was about the same time he
met my mother, got married, and started having children.
At some point, he even became a truck driver to pick up
extra cash. Back then they did not have the same laws and
regulations, so he would exceed today's rules on how

many hours a truck driver could work. At the end of the day, my father did not want his kids experiencing poverty like he did.

I like to talk about money management because it is really interesting to me. It is interesting to me because so many people are really not educated on the matter. You can make a great salary, but without knowledge of how to manage your money, you could quickly fail and lose most, if not all of what you've earned. I truly believe my grandpa was a very hard worker. The wages were not great at the time until Jimmy Hoffa came into the picture and forced better pay through unions. This was roughly in the 50's or 60's, when Jimmy Hoffa began the Teamsters. After that point, my grandpa began making more money. Unfortunately, this was much later in his career near his retirement.

As I mentioned in the first chapter, the current events do truly play a role on your current situation. We must pay attention to the current events and make sure we are making good decisions by keeping current events in mind. Never take a chance because you are lazy. Put effort into fully understanding the situation and make decisions based on the whole picture. A little work upfront to gain background information can save you much more work afterwards. A bad decision can create much more work for you, which is why we need to focus on getting it right the first time.

Annual trends are important to your budget and you can go as deep as you want into the trending. Staying too close to the surface may allow you to miss crucial information, which is why you should dive as deep as you can. The table here shows 2009 to 2019 salary increase of 3%, 4%, and 5% per year. This exercise is to show you what a difference in just 1% or 2% more would make over an 11-year stretch.

Salary Increases

Year	0% increase	3% increase	4% increase	5% increase
2009	$50,000.00	$50,000.00	$50,000.00	$50,000.00
2010	$50,000.00	$51,500.00	$52,000.00	$52,500.00
2011	$50,000.00	$53,045.00	$54,080.00	$55,125.00
2012	$50,000.00	$54,636.35	$56,243.20	$57,881.25
2013	$50,000.00	$56,275.44	$58,492.93	$60,775.31
2014	$50,000.00	$57,963.70	$60,832.65	$63,814.08
2015	$50,000.00	$59,702.61	$63,265.95	$67,004.78
2016	$50,000.00	$61,493.69	$65,796.59	$70,355.02
2017	$50,000.00	$63,338.50	$68,428.45	$73,872.77
2018	$50,000.00	$65,238.66	$71,165.59	$77,566.41
2019	$50,000.00	$67,195.82	$74,012.21	$81,444.73
Total	$550,000	$640,389.78	$674,317.57	$710,339.36

At a 3% increase, you are earning $640,389 over 11-years. At a 4% increase, you are earning $674,317.57 over 11-years. At a 5% increase, you are earning $710,339.36 over 11-years. This is much more than earning the same amount over the 11-years, which ends up being $550,000. This is $90,389.78 less than a 3% increase and $160,339.36 less than a 5% increase, year over year. Think about all the things you could do with an extra $90,000 to $160,000. In the first couple of years, a 3% to 5% increase in salary only gives you an extra $1,000 or $2,000 per year, depending on what increase you get. It is after a few years where you start realizing, the extra 3% to 5% increase on your salary each year is really adding up.

Here is a chart, which illustrates my point. From 2009 to 2019, you are not seeing much difference between 0% to 5% increase in salary. In fact, it all looks pretty much the same. It is not until you take the total where you can see a significant difference. This chart was created from the table of data we just went over. So, you can see the graph matches up with the table. The total of 0%, 3%, 4%, and 5%, are $550,000, $640,389.78, $674,317.57, and $710,339.36, respectively. As years pass and you continue to generate small gains, those gains add up to large gains.

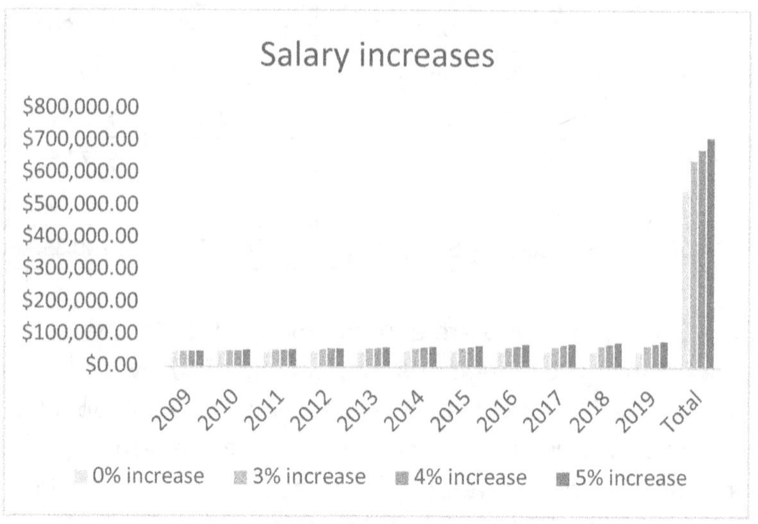

Outside of the financial world, you can use small gains in other areas you are focusing on too. A great example would be school. Procrastination is really harmful to our journey to success. When we procrastinate, we are letting time pass and putting extra pressure on ourselves to utilize a small amount of time to get everything done that we need to complete. We leave no room for error and a lot of times we just won't have enough time to perform at an acceptable level. By using the small gains method, we are going to utilize all time allotted to us. This means from the get-go we are going to start creating a plan and execute that plan. We are only hurting ourselves by not taking advantage of all time available to us for our efforts to meet our goals.

In school, we are expected to consume a lot of knowledge in a very short period of time. We should use our time wisely and plan to take small chunks of that information frequently. Some say, you should study for shorter periods of time and have small breaks in between. This allows your brain to get some fresh air and not burn up in the process. I personally start day dreaming if I am studying too long, especially when I am not super interested in the topic I am studying. I get to a point where my brain just won't take in any new information. I personally need to take the small breaks or I'll go insane.

If you have an exam every 4 weeks on 4 chapters, I'd recommend getting the 4 chapters mastered in the first 3 weeks and use the final week for review. This would require you to learn 1.33 chapters per week in the first 3 weeks. If you divide this up into a week, you are to learn roughly 25% of the materials each day for the 1.33 chapters per week. This is based on work days only, so 5 days per week. If you include the extra 2 days for weekends, then you are expected to study even less content per day. Week to week, the table titled **Study Schedule** shows what your study schedule may look like in preparation for the exam.

In the first week, all of the first chapter should be completed and partial of chapter two. In the second week, all of chapter one, chapter two, and partial of chapter three should be completed. In the third week, all of chapter one, two, three, and four should be completed. This allows you to spend the fourth week reviewing.

Study Schedule

	Week 1	Week 2	Week 3	Week 4
Chapter 1	100%	100%	100%	REVIEW
Chapter 2	33%	100%	100%	REVIEW
Chapter 3	0%	33%	100%	REVIEW
Chapter 4	0%	0%	100%	REVIEW

This is not the only way of breaking it apart. Keep in mind, your plan should fit your personal preferences and schedule. It is very possible that you need to break into the fourth week to complete chapter four. If this works for you, then do it that way. The point here is to have a plan going in and make sure you are utilizing all time provided the best you can. It only hurts us when we procrastinate. It is better to over prepare, than under prepare. I've been known to over prepare when I have to present, especially to big audiences or audiences with people who I deem as important.

When we talk small gains, we can also talk about our careers in terms of roles. From college, I took a role as a chemist for a startup pharmaceutical company. The company was extremely small and not the ideal place for me because the pay was super low. I spent three years working as a chemist before I left. The next stop was in maintenance for a fortune 500 company, making more money. I spent 6 months in maintenance and then went to the packaging department. Once I was in the packaging department, I spent several years supporting various business units. I ended up learning about various types of packaging such as steel and aluminum cans, plastic bottles, cups, bowls, corrugate, various films, pouches, and so on. I also gained business acumen and project management skills.

At each role, I picked up new knowledge from a wide range of experiences. Typically, anytime I moved into a new role my salary increased. Even if the increase was not huge, it was something. I also was building my resume with each move. Keep in mind, we cannot just go into a role, do nothing, and move on. We need to produce results, to show others we are adding value. Why else would an employer want us? We must add value. Our employer is providing us a salary for our service. We are also networking and building our brand.

As a packaging engineer, I was responsible for producing $1 million in savings per year for the business unit I supported. I can assure you I was not making $1 million per year as a packaging engineer. Quite often, the expected return on our service does not match the salary we receive. The employer will always want a higher return than the salary they are paying. To make the most of our time, we need to put our best effort in at all times. We should also be grateful we have a job because there are plenty of people who are unemployed. There are plenty of people living in poverty. To have a job, we are fortunate and need to keep this in mind.

The small gains method would require you to continuously push for higher salary and lower expense each year. We should not get caught up with feelings of 'not getting enough' or feeling 'others are getting more than you'. Focus on your own gains from year to year and focus on how you can personally improve. We can take in other people's performance for quick comparison, but do not focus solely on this aspect. In fact, make this comparison to other people's performance very minimal because your comparison to yourself is what really matters. Not everyone plays on the same playing field. This is important to understand.

In college, I remember being in difficult courses such as physical chemistry and advanced inorganic chemistry. There were a lot of discussions between classmates about how difficult the class was. Some students would even ask how well others did, to justify their mediocre grades. Just because the entire class is not doing well, does not mean you have to do poorly too. We need to act like leaders and not hide behind other's poor performance. After college, in the real world when you start your career, there is no bell curve in performance. You are completely accountable for your own performance and will not be able to count on a bell curve to pull your performance up.

If my father decided to justify his poor situation as a child by relating himself to the other poor kids in his neighborhood, then I could have also had a poor childhood. The fact is, he did not accept a lower standard of living. He worked very hard to achieve success and provide a very good living situation for his children. It was his hard work that elevated his family to the next level. At times he was working two full time jobs. He was willing to do this to provide better opportunities for his family. This state of mind did not change even as he did get out of poverty. This type of thinking trickled down to me, when we started our personal business building equipment. At the time my father did not need the extra cash. I now realize he was doing it more for me than himself.

I could have continued achieving my degree in college, started my career, and been fine. Since I am my father's son and have many of the same ideas he does, I was not content with the bare minimum. I wanted more for myself and for my family. I started working on small gains since my freshman year in college. At the time, I did not know I was doing it or why I was doing it. The important thing is, I was consistent and carried on, even when times were tough. Overtime, my tortoise mindset did end up working for me. As mentioned, you may be a hare or tortoise, depending on your stamina. The reason I distance myself from the hare characteristics is because the hare is not as consistent as the tortoise. A tortoise is slow and steady, so in the long run, the tortoise should beat the hare.

I will say if you do move too slowly, you may not have enough time in your lifetime to meet all of your goals. This is a fine line you need to balance. Too fast and you could wear yourself out too soon. Too slow and you may never reach your goals. This is a challenge I've struggled with, but for me small gains makes sense. As long as I am pushing daily to gain results, overtime these results will add up. I believe the challenges come when someone is not doing anything for days, weeks, or months. Then it becomes difficult to catch up. If too much time passes by, then you may not even try catching up if you feel it is too late. A lot of this is psychological and we need to make sure we are not letting our fears get in our way of our successes.

I think about everything I have today and realize it did not all come to me overnight. My college degrees, house, vehicles, friends, family, and so on. All of these things did not happen overnight. My bachelors degree in biochemistry and masters degree in packaging took over 6-years alone. This does not include all the schooling leading up to that point. Paying off my mortgage will have taken 8-years, which is very fast. It took 6-years to get married, which is the time from meeting my wife to marrying her. It took another 3-years to have our first child. 2-years after our first, we had another child. We must remain patient.

One of the biggest lessons my father has taught me in my life is to be patient. In a way, his teachings have led me to approaching goals by using small gains. Without patience, I would not have been able to allow myself to put effort into making small gains along the way. Think about the goals you want to achieve and the criteria you need to accomplish those goals. Think about how you can best utilize your time today and tomorrow, to move toward achieving those goals. Each day that goes by is a day you can use to push forward and get closer to reaching your goals. Step back and look at the big picture from start to finish. This is the type of mindset you need to be successful. Think small gains. Think consistency. Think stamina over a long period of time and you will achieve great results.

My mother lived in Santiago, Chile for the first twenty years of her life. My mother's family was well-off during this time. Her father (my grandpa) was a CFO of an electronics company and owned several businesses, including a book store in downtown Santiago. Life was good! In 1970, Salvador Allende won presidency and stayed in office until 1973. He was classified as a democratic socialist, but my family always said he was simply a communist. This is where the story takes a turn for the worst.

In 1970, when Allende became President of Chile, things dramatically changed for my mother and her family. Her mother, father, two sisters, brother, and her were forced to live differently after Allende took over the country. A change in attitude swept throughout Chile. My mother's family had several maids who started stealing from them. When confronted, the maids responded by saying, Allende says we can have anything you have. My mother's family was always good to their maids, so this was very surprising. These maids were dismissed from their duties because they could no longer be trusted.

Roughly, during the same time, burglars jumped the gates of my mother's house in Chile to burglarize them in the middle of the night. My grandfather gathered everyone into one room and gave my mother, who was the oldest of all her siblings, a gun for protection. My mother was nervous and did not want to use it. Fortunately, the burglars had enough sense to flee upon hearing my grandfather run out after them. During those years, countless people mysteriously ended up dead. My mother's family refused to join the communist party, so they needed to purchase food illegally through the black market. This was very risky and could have had serious legal implications if caught.

Also, during this time, people were constantly stealing from my grandfather's book store in downtown Santiago, Chile. Due to these political issues, his business was facing enormous challenges. Much of what took my grandfather years to build up, was quickly falling within a fraction of that time it took to build. Chile no longer felt like home to my mother's family. They needed to look elsewhere for a better life. This was a very difficult decision. They would need to decide whether they were going to stay in the midst of the political turmoil or move far away to another country and leave everything they've ever known behind.

On September 11, 1973, Salvador Allende committed suicide with an AK-47 that he received as a gift from Fidel Castro. Due to the horrific events during those years, my mother's family did not want to stick around. Even with Allende out of power, there would be too much uncertainty in Chile and my mother's family did not want to risk anymore hardship. Additionally, during the years Allende was president, they took a huge financial hit. This was their chance to start over somewhere else. If another communist leader like Allende took over again, my family may not be as fortunate. Another leader like Allende could cripple what was left of my family and their finances.

At the time, Australia and Canada were accepting immigrants from Chile. My mother's family decided to move to Canada because they knew a few friends who had already took this journey. From what they heard, Canada was a pretty nice place to live with good people. The government was also stable in comparison to Chile at the time. Unfortunately, my mother's family would end up losing the remainder of their fortune when they moved. They would not have time to sell their house, book store, or any of the other assets. My grandfather confided in a business partner from the past to help liquidate his assets. The expectation was to receive payment after the person sold his assets. My grandfather never saw a cent.

My mother's childhood is very polarizing from my father's childhood. My father lived in poverty while my mother had maids, lived in a luxurious house, went skiing in the Andes mountains, and vacationed at some of the nicest beaches in South America. At one point, they had a beach house next to Julio Iglesias. My mother used to tell me stories of women hanging off of Julio Iglesias' deck, which faced the beach. I could just imagine girls in their bathing suits climbing up the side of the deck from the beach, attempting to get a glimpse of Julio sunbathing on a lay flat beach chair on his deck.

At about the same time my mother was living the high life, my father couldn't even play baseball or own a baseball glove. I mean, what was the cost of a baseball glove back then? Maybe a few dollars? My father lived on the east end of Chatham and went to John McGregor high school. My mother went to the Grange School located in Santiago Chile, which is a British school for the wealthy. My mother told me Queen Elizabeth even went to visit the Grange School back in the 1960's. My mother and all of her classmates stood in a long line in the hallway, while the

Queen walked by. It was a very big deal for the school and of course, my mother.

The events of the 1970's turned my mother's family upside down. Once my mother and her family arrived in Chatham, Ontario, they immediately got jobs. My mother went from having house-keepers to being a house-keeper at a local motel. My mother and her siblings also got seasonal jobs picking tomatoes in the field and did some work at a local food manufacturing plant. My grandfather also got a job in this plant where they were making ketchup. Still till this day, my grandfather will not eat ketchup. He said there were too many flies and insects cooked in with the tomatoes. The entire process grossed him out and he just could not bring himself to eat ketchup. I can relate because I've seen a lot of products being manufactured and it isn't always pretty.

This new town was very different for them. Santiago, Chile was a big city and that is what they were used to. Now they are living in a small town where it gets extremely cold in the winters. The people are different too. Typical small-town folk can be overwhelming, especially when you came from a large city where nobody says 'hello'. It can be quite strange when everyone greets you with a smile, even if you do not know them. Although my mother's family knew English, their primary language was Spanish. This too required some effort to get used to speaking more English than Spanish. Although my mother's family knew English well, things are called different things in different regions. The best example I can think of is pop versus soda versus soda pop. Depending on where you are, this drink could be called multiple things. Some places just call it Dr. Pepper no matter what drink you are drinking.

As much as people will say, money is not important. I strongly feel money has a huge impact on what you can and cannot do in life. I agree that money should not be everything, but we do need to understand it does have control over us on a daily basis. My mother's family became financially unstable and were vulnerable, living in a new country with very little money. Extra money would have certainly helped the transition go a little bit smoother. When we struggle, it can help us appreciate the little things we once took for granted. At one point, my mother's family could eat any luxurious food they wanted. After moving to Canada, they needed to be a little more selective about what foods they bought because money was tight.

At one point when my mother was cleaning rooms, her boss at the time was stealing her tips. A few dollars here and a few dollars there does not seem like much, but for my mother it was a lot. This type of situation can leave you feeling powerless and not very good about yourself or your employer. My mother did not give up and continued going to college to work her way up to a better job. I am very proud of her for this. One thing President Allende could not take away was family. I believe my mother's family made it through the difficult time because they had each other. They would always stick together and have been stronger because of it.

My mother had an uncle living in Quebec during this time who also came from Chile. He started at IBM as a janitor. He ended up getting a job in the same building for IBM as the elevator operator. Through this job he was able to get to know many of the senior management team who saw something in him. They helped him get back into school to earn a degree. He ended up working his way up through the ranks all the way to Vice President and did very well for himself. Sadly, he had a heart attack years later on his yacht. This is the type of success story that makes me feel good. It shows us that everyone has an opportunity to do well.

There are many countries today like Chile, where poor people are just always going to be poor. I have been told this about parts of India, Russia, Africa, and so on. There are many parts of the world where you will never improve your quality of life because you'd never get the opportunity. For example, if you are working as a factory worker in one of these countries, you are barely making enough money to survive. You'd never get the chance to go to school and better yourself because you are too busy trying to make ends meet. In the United States and Canada, everyone truly does have the opportunity to do better. In Canada and the USA, we are fortunate to have opportunities to grow and improve our lives. I have met countless people who have done this. My mother's uncle was one of them who went from the bottom to the top because of his hard work. That makes me proud of him.

I would say we are hearing fewer stories like my mother's uncle's story at IBM where he started as a janitor and moved up to vice president. The reason is because more people are not staying at the same company for too long. There are a lot of these millennial types, like me that will jump around for a better title and pay. It also feels as if companies are not as loyal to their employees as they once were. My father has been with the same company for thirty-five years. Although they were good to him for many years, are they still good to him today? I'd let him answer that for himself. At the end of the day we need to do what is best for ourselves and our families. Fewer companies are offering pensions today, which also does not help keep good employees around. The workplace today is vastly different from 10-years ago, 15-years ago, 20-years ago, and so on.

If you haven't figured out by now, my mother and father met in my hometown Chatham. My father was not my mother's type to say the least. At the time they met, my father had a perm because Jack the barber was going back to school to learn new types of haircuts and offered my dad free cuts for a year, if he could give my dad a perm. This was the same Jack that gave my father a job at 12-years old sweeping up his shop. My father also wore a lot of flannels back in those days and always had jeans on. He was also a heavy drinker. My mother on the other hand did not like the perm, flannels, jeans, or heavy drinking. Her ex-boyfriend Philip in Chile was basically a replica of Julio Iglesias and that was the type of guy she was looking for. Since she was in Chatham, she was probably not going to find that guy, which is how she ended up with my father.

Without going into much detail, my mother and father ended up getting married, having two children, and lived happily ever after. There wedding was about $1,200 and not too glamorous from what I was told. When it comes to weddings, the more money you spend does not mean your marriage will last longer. My parents have been happily married for over 35 years. Similarly, my wife and I had a nice wedding, but didn't out-do ourselves and break the bank. I wanted to pay for our own wedding, just like my parents did and we did just that. We could have spent a ton of money on our wedding, but what does that prove? We still had to spend a considerable amount of money, but not too much where we are still in debt. We ended up paying cash for everything to make sure we did not end up in debt because of our wedding.

Both my parents have worked extremely hard to give my older brother and me everything. They wanted better for their children, as I'd want better for my children. The way to get your children there is to provide them with opportunities. This is exactly what my parents did for us. From the start, when my brother and I misbehaved, they did not yell and hit us. They sat us down and explained why we were wrong and how we could fix it. I have great respect for my parents and they always made me feel as if they had great respect for me. They genuinely care about my feelings and make me feel special. This is what I want to do for my children. This type of corrective action allowed for my brother and I to take the opportunity to think about what we did. It allowed us to self-correct and take ownership for our actions. We did not change our actions out of fear.

Instilling fear in your children will only make them adjust when you are around. When you are not around, the fear leaves and they will continue being bad around others. At the same time, I do not want my children to fear me. I want us to see eye to eye and have a mutual understanding. I'd want to make sure my children are thinkers and problem solvers. My parents allowed my brother and myself the opportunity to be thinkers and problem solvers. I cannot speak for my brother, but I do feel I am a thinker and problem solver. This is the way I function and it works perfect for me.

When I am at the shop building equipment with my father, I often like to learn about his family and his childhood experiences. I want to know where he came from and what matters most to him. I love hearing about the wild adventures he had when he was a kid and no, he was not the most innocent kid. He ended up getting into a lot of trouble, but things were different back then. He could have ended up in jail for some of the things they did, if it were today. I always laugh when he tells me the story about when they left a friend hanging from a window because the kid's fingers were pinched in the window. Supposedly, the kid was locked out of his house and a good deed of trying to help him back in, ended up being a cruel practical joke. My father and his friends lifted this poor kid up to an open window. While this friend was pulling up to get into the window, the window shut on his fingers. This is when my father and his friends fled the scene, leaving the kid hanging there. It is pretty cruel.

The story about my father and his friends shoving hamburgers in their friend's couches at a birthday party is also a favorite. I guess the kid's mother was not a great cook and burned all the burgers. Instead of throwing them into the garbage, my father and his friends thought it was funnier to shove them between couch cushions. The mother was not pleased when she found them weeks later.

There was also the story about my father and his friends shooting a rifle at a car illegally parked. They shot the tires out to teach the guy a lesson in hopes he would never illegally park in front of their house again. The sad thing is, the car belonged to an elderly couple visiting their son a few doors down. It did not belong to the same young guy who illegally parked in that spot every other weekend. My father and his friends quickly hid because they did not want to get caught.

The time I've spent with my father at the shop is priceless. In this world, money is important because it is the currency, we use to purchase things including food and water. Would we make the same decisions, if money was not in the equation? Most likely not, but we must understand money is 9 out of 10 times going to be in our equation for decision-making. I am so proud of my parents for their hard work. I would not be where I am today without them. Their goal was to create a nice life for their children, meaning my brother and me. Although they were probably not thinking directly about money, we know money has some part of it.

Then, there will be times when you make a decision based on money and you realize, it was not the right decision. As a child, I did not see my father as much as I would have liked to. He was not out drinking, partying, or anything like that. He was working and working some more. For a very long time, he spent much of his time working to make money. He was very focused on providing for his family and making sure we were getting everything we needed. For the first 7 or 8 years of my life, my father worked 6 to 7 days per week. If my father had a day off, it was a very big deal for my brother and me.

There was a point when my mother was working after my brother was born. This was early in my brother's life, when he was being watched by my aunt. My brother ended up falling down the stairs and needing stitches in his head. My father picked up my brother, took him to the hospital for stitches, and then took my brother into my mother's work. My mother at the time wanted to work, but my father wanted my mother to stay home and watch my brother. In some way, this was an opportunity for my father to show my mother she should watch my brother full-time instead of working. My mother was horrified and immediately quit her job to watch my brother.

I was born 2 years after this incident and was always watched by my mother. I guess the accident was bad enough to persuade my mother to stay home with my brother. This also explains why my father felt like he had to work so much. I do question whether he could have worked a little bit less to spend more time with my brother and me. Then again, I know he was doing it to help support his family the best way he knew how. He also wanted to make sure my brother and me could play baseball, go on field trips, and participate in anything else we desired. He did not want money being the limiting factor.

The longest stretch of time my father was away for work was when I was 14 years old. One of the factories in Texas went on strike, so they flew my father down to help keep the factory running. My father was gone for 6 weeks without coming home. This was the longest I went without seeing my father and I did not like it. It was also a very scary time for him because the people on strike were not happy with people like my father from the corporate office who kept the factory going. A lot of people in Texas have guns and my father thought someone could confront him at his hotel or in town where he would eat. He did not sleep too well for the 6 weeks he spent in Texas. When he got back, they asked if he wanted to do a second stretch of time down in Texas and surprisingly, he said 'no'. This was a relief for my family because we loved having him home.

Now that I have children, I do my best to support them financially, but have learned I need to spend quality time with them too. I do not want to miss their childhood because I wanted to make a few extra dollars. When I am at work, I do work hard. When I'm home with them, I do my best to pay full attention to them and make the experience a positive one. I avoid from diverting my attention to my phone. I avoid from diverting my attention to the TV. I want to solely focus on them, and I want them to see me happy at all times. I leave my troubles outside the door because my family does not need to be burdened by issues I should deal with outside of the house.

As you can see, both my father and mother had troublesome times in their life, which motivated them to work hard in hopes of providing their children with greater opportunities. I often reflect on this because it is super meaningful to me. It is incredible to think that my parents cared so much for my brother and me, that they would sacrifice so much, to give us the opportunity for a better life. It was not the guarantee for a better life. It was the opportunity for a better life. There is a very big difference between guarantee and opportunity. A guaranteed better life would mean my brother and I would not need to do anything. The better life would be provided. An opportunity for a better life means we actually have to do something.

So, yes, we had a very nice childhood, but it was up to us to go further. It was our decision to take opportunities given to us and make the best of them. I truly believe this is exactly what I've done and am doing each day. I've worked hard to complete school. I've worked hard to grow in my career. I've worked hard to stay in good shape by going to the gym. I've worked hard to continually learn, so I can use newly learned skillsets for further growth in my career. I've also worked hard to be the best father I can be. An opportunity is only as good as the effort you are willing to give towards that opportunity.

My college advisor once told me, that I needed to come with passion, or he would not be able to help me. This was the first time anyone ever said anything like this to me. First of all, I never thought of myself as impassionate until that day. I did a quick self-assessment and came to the realization that I was not super passionate when it came to school. This was the point in my college career when I told myself, I would need to be more passionate about school. This advice from my college advisor is still one of the best pieces of advice anyone has ever given me. Quite simply, without passion you are not going to be able to achieve some of those more challenging goals.

When I think about the amazing stories my parents have both told me, I often think about the stories I could one day tell my children. Will my stories be as amazing as my parents? It is challenging to compete with my parents' childhood stories because their stories are simply amazing.

I would often wonder how my dad in particular could be so patient with my brother and me. But then I'd remember, some of the issues he'd face in his life were so great, almost anything my brother and I could do, would not compare. On the other hand, my mother could be a little bit less patient with us. But she is from a different background and at the end of the day, has always been a great mother. Her expectations were much higher from that of my father. I look at this too, as a positive thing.

When you look at yourself, your parents, your siblings, your cousins, aunts, uncles, grandparents, and other family members, what do you see? Who taught you what? How did these people impact your life? Much of what I know today did come from family members. I can still remember when I was 5 or 6-years old when my Uncle Chris first taught me how to hand scissors to someone. He told me to grab the sharp end and give them the handle, so they would not get cut. Simple things like this travel a far distance. My grandfather (mother's dad), taught me to talk about the good times and not reminisce about the bad times. He also taught me many things on educate such as how to pour wine at the table.

My grandpa (mother's father) who we call 'Papi' is a major foundation for my family and deserves great respect. Similarly, my grandpa (father's father) who worked hard his whole life, deserves great respect too. Sadly he passed away when I was young and I did not get much time with him. I did not know my grandmothers from both my father and mother's side too well. I actually never met my father's mother because she passed away before I was even born. I only knew my mother's mother for a few years before she passed away. I wish I could have known my father's mother and father better. I wish I could have known my mother's mother better. They would have taught me so much and I would have cherished those moments. The next best thing is talking to my parents about their mothers and fathers. Family history is important to me.

My brother has taught me too much to recap here. He is somebody I've spent countless time with since I was born. He was my first friend and longest friend. He taught me how to pitch, even though I never made it to the big leagues like Fergie Jenkinson or Billy Atkinson. He taught me how to play the guitar, introduced me to good music, put me in his films, and so much more. I observed him when he made good decisions and bad decisions. The good decisions, I try to mimic. The bad decisions, I try to avoid. At my wedding, he was my best man and did the most amazing best man speech ever. It included him singing, *Through the Years*, which is a song by Kenny Rogers. I'm still out on the verdict whether this was a good or bad decision.

I'd recommend you take some time to reflect on your past and your family's past. I'd recommend you learn as much as you can about your family's history and where you came from. A lot of this can help predict your future. If your parents have traits you do not like, then think about yourself and if you are also following in their footsteps. Are you exhibiting signs of those unattractive traits? If so, do your best to work on a plan to correct it. A trait I've seen in my family is procrastination on certain things. My family are hard workers but do procrastinate when it comes to working on some of the bigger picture things. This is why I often take a step back and look at things at a high level. We need the ability to zoom in and zoom out at different points. We cannot always be working in the weeds. We occasionally need to zoom out and see the bigger picture, so we can be more strategic. These are things we all need to think about.

Family will always be a number one priority for me. I have realized that you do need to sacrifice time and work to earn money to support your family. As much as I'd love to stay home all day with my wife, children, cat, and dog, I simply know this is not feasible. I need to build a solid financial foundation to support the needs of my family. My wife also works and is also helping with this effort. When my sons want to play a sport, go on a field trip, or need money for some other activity, I want to have the cash ready. I'd never want to deny my sons an opportunity simply because I did not have the money. My mother and father worked very hard to provide my brother and I with countless opportunities. I want to do the same for my sons because this is very important to me.

I am 34 years old and have several years left before retirement. However, I do not want to approach retirement age and not have enough money to retire. Sounds pretty simple or at least you'd think it is. Worse yet, I do not want to approach retirement age and have debt. Too many people today do approach retirement age with a considerable amount of debt. We all know time flies, yet we keep telling ourselves we will get our financial situation in order one day. That day never does come, and we are forced to work longer than we planned. This is not a situation I want to be in, which is why I am planning in advance.

 The first thing we want to do is determine what age we want to retire and how much money we need for retirement. Picking a retirement age is the easy part. Understanding how much money you need at that age for retirement is the challenging part because it requires us to estimate how long we will live. One factor that complicates retirement calculations is debt and this is why you should work on eliminating debt as quickly as possible. Without debt, you are going to have less stress and be able to manage your finances more clearly. To simplify the retirement calculations, I've used a method that takes debt completely out of the equation.

There are two tables I created to help organize the quick calculation on how much money you will need for retirement. Again, this calculation is simple when using Microsoft Excel or an equivalent spreadsheet software program. Using Excel or an equivalent will allow you to play with the numbers and assess different situations with ease. This helps us get a grasp how varying numbers will affect the outcome. It is good to play with the numbers to see what results are produced using different numbers. You will see what I mean when you get to the retirement tables.

In the first table titled **Retirement Age Information**, I have the first row 'age at 0% debt'. As mentioned, we are going to start this calculation at the age you no longer have any debt. This helps get rid of the complicated interest and other fees that may be included when having debt. The second row 'planned retirement age' is the age you plan on retiring at. The third row 'years left to retirement' is the 'planned retirement age' minus 'age at 0% debt'. In other words, how long do you have until you retire from the age you reach 0% debt. Fourth row 'final age' is the age you plan on living until. It could be called 'death age' too, but I think that sounds morbid. The fifth row 'years in retirement' is 'final age' minus 'planned retirement age'. Basically, how many years will you be retired and need to withdraw money from your retirement fund.

Retirement Age Information

Age at 0% debt	38
Planned retirement age	60
Years left to retirement 'planned retirement age' – 'age at 0% debt'	22
Final age	100
Years in retirement 'final age' – planned retirement age'	40

The next table titled **Retirement Financial Information**, I speak more about the money aspect. The first row is the cash value you have at the age you are debt-free. This cash could be 401(k), mutual funds, saved cash, Roth IRA, and so on. Basically, any type of cash you have for retirement can be included in this section. I would exclude any assets such as a house, car, boat, and so on. The reason I would exclude these is because they are not liquid funds that you can withdraw from at any time. It is possible to sell and produce cash from these assets, but there is a level of uncertainty of the actual value of each asset. I'd simply not rely on the assets as part of your retirement fund. This keeps things simple and realistic.

The second row 'budget per year in retirement' is the amount of money you require when you are living in your retirement years. You would need to understand your cost of living and how much money you will need each year after retirement. Since you will have no debt, you would only need to think about food, utilities, taxes, medical costs, and entertainment costs to name a few. To be safe, after calculating your budget you'd require after retirement, you should add an extra 10%. This will help account for inflation and any other unexpected costs.

The third row 'estimated value required at retirement' is 'years in retirement' multiplied by 'budget per year in retirement'. This gives you the total budget you will need to survive financially in your retirement years. The fourth row 'required earnings per year until retirement' is the 'estimated value required at retirement' minus 'current value at 0% debt' divided by 'years left to retirement'. This gives you the amount of money you will need to put aside each year starting when you reach 0% debt, until you retire.

Retirement Financial Information

Current value at 0% debt	$100,000.00
Budget per year in retirement	$35,000.00
Estimated value required at retirement 'years in retirement' x 'budget per year in retirement'	$1,400,000.00
Required earnings per year until retirement ('estimated value required at retirement' – 'current value at 0% debt')/ ('years in retirement')	$59,090.91

I cannot emphasize enough the importance of getting all debt removed as quickly as you can, so you can start saving up for retirement. The Federal Reserve Board says over one-third of homeowners between 65 and 74 years old still have a mortgage with an average balance of $118,000. It is quite possible these people have a bunch of money saved up, but I would get nervous having over $100,000 in debt at those ages. With 0% debt, you have a much better debt to income ratio. Debt-to-income ratio is defined as the percentage of your gross monthly income that goes to paying your monthly debt payments.

To calculate your debt-to-income ratio, you would follow this equation below:

$$\frac{total\ monthly\ debt}{monthly\ gross\ income} \times 100 = debt\ to\ income\ ratio$$

Total monthly debt includes all payments going out each month such as mortgage, student loans, auto loans, credit cards, and so on. Monthly gross income is your income before taxes.

There are countless articles on the internet defining what an acceptable debt-to-income ratio looks like. When I look at debts, I understand we will always have some sort of debt as long as we are using credit cards or have some sort of utility bill. There is a difference between having long-term debt and short-term debt that you pay off at the end of the month. A long-term debt incurs interest and can be quite costly. A short-term debt that you pay off at the end of the month should not incur interest, which is acceptable in my opinion, as long as you manage it well.

Short-term debt or credit card debt must be paid at the end of each monthly cycle and there should never be any exceptions to this rule. This is a very strict rule I have, especially when a lot of times credit card interest can be as high as 25%. On a $100 charge, you are paying $25 for each year you don't pay it off. Now imagine the charge was $1,000. On the same 25% APR (annual percentage rate), you are paying $250 in interest for every year it is not paid. There are people that have upwards of $10,000 in debt to a credit card with 25% APR and their annual interest charge is $2,500. If they end up not being able to pay the $10,000 off, they are now continuously paying $2,500 over several years. After two years, they are now over $5,000 in interest. This means, they are now paying $15,000 for something that was originally $10,000.

Sadly, some people don't even remember what they bought by the time they pay off their credit card bill. This becomes more concerning and is very problematic. Purchasing little knick-knacks can end up costing you more than you think. Try and catch yourself the next time you say, it's only a few dollars. Think about how many times you've done this and how much money you've spent on stuff you do not need. You are not required to purchase products anytime you leave the house. More importantly, you are not required to purchase products anytime you surf the web. Control your spend to make sure you don't go into debt foolishly.

If we want to get to retirement relatively quickly, we are going to need to set retirement goals and create a plan to get there. We cannot pay any extra money towards unnecessary interest, fees, or charges because this will only end up slowing us down. We need to make sure we are controlling our credit cards and limit usage on each one. We need to think big picture. We are now at a point in our life where we need to really think about whether we should be purchasing a bunch of items that add no value in our life. If you lack control in this department, you can try this trick. Never purchase anything you want for 24 hours. This means if you are out and see something you want, wait at least a full day to purchase it. This may give you enough time to figure out if you really need it or not.

If we think back 10, 15, 20 years ago, we would see e-commerce was not as prevalent as it is today. Today, every major retailer has an online store where you can shop 24/7. Instead of having to get into your car and drive down to the store during certain hours, you can now hop online in the comfort of your own home, and purchase goods and services at all hours of the day. It is both marvelous and horrendous at the same time. When you are up late at night with nothing to do and get bored, you are more likely to shop online to keep yourself entertained. Years ago, this was not the case. Today, who doesn't go onto Amazon.com and purchase frivolous things?

A few years back, I went to my friend's house and he shows me this doorbell looking device next to his baby's crib. He said this button was linked directly to Amazon and he could purchase diapers every time that button was clicked. He did not need to sign online and spend time shopping for diapers. Purchasing new diapers for his baby was just a click away. This is absolutely insane because I could go in there and start hitting the button randomly. In 2-days he would have a bunch of diapers show up at his front door that I ordered. In my opinion, it has gotten too easy to purchase products. The availability of new products to the masses is unbelievable. In today's world, there are too many temptations and I believe this is a very big problem.

The same friend with the doorbell also bought his Tesla Model 3 with a click of a button. He visited the Tesla website, selected the car he wanted, put down a deposit, and in a few weeks his car showed up. As awesome as his Tesla is, I question whether people can handle this new responsibility. Believe me, I love Teslas and love the fact that you don't need to deal with car salesman. The part that scares me is that everything is incredibly easy to purchase online. I've jumped onto the Tesla website multiple times myself and was very tempted to purchase one. I probably went onto the website at least fifteen to twenty times before I restricted myself from visiting again. I told myself I could not purchase a new car until I was out of debt. I was aiming to pay off all debt before purchasing a new car. I would save up enough cash and purchase my next car without a loan.

I can even think back to around 2008 when the housing market crashed. Banks were giving out excessive mortgages to people who could clearly not afford them. It may be true that some of these people did not know they could not afford the mortgage. It would be very surprising to them when they lost their house at some point a few years later. Ignorance is a poor excuse when it comes to financial matters. We need to educate ourselves as best as we can before making any big financial decision. We cannot just hope the decision turns out good. I also see the mortgages around the housing market crash as being too readily available. People are naturally going to take whatever they can, especially when it is money.

As shown previously in this chapter, I've laid out two tables. One table based on retirement age and the other table based on retirement funding. Using these tables, we are able to layout some criteria around our planned retirement age and cash availability for our retirement. As mentioned in chapter 2, we need to understand our starting point, end point, and challenges in between. For the purposes of this discussion, the starting point will be your age at 0% debt. The end point would be the start of your retirement age. The challenges would include struggles to get your required earnings per year until retirement.

In our example, the required earnings per year until retirement is $59,090.91. This is the amount you are required to contribute to your retirement fund on average per year. So, once you hit 0% debt, you are going to have to put aside on average $59,090.91 per year for 22 years. As the table shows, the age at 0% debt is 38 years old and the planned retirement age is 60 years old. You would have 22 years to save up the $1.4 million required for retirement. Remember, at 0% debt age we already have

$100,000 saved up. This means you will only need to save up another $1.3 million for retirement. When you divide the $1.3 million by 22 years, you get $59,090.91.

In the next 22 years, are you going to have enough money to put aside $59,090.91 per year on average? If you are putting money into a 401(k), then you would expect your money to earn interest. If you place the original $100,000 saved into a mutual fund or equivalent that earns 7.5% interest per year on average and add $20,000 per year, we would end up with $1.5 million in 22 years. This is another way of looking at your retirement plan.

Using excel, you can easily calculate compound interest using the following formula:

=FV(rate,nper,pmt,[pv],[type])

where,

rate – interest rate per period
nper – total number of payment periods
pmt – payment made each period (entered as negative number)
pv – (optional) present value of future payments
type – (optional) when payments are due

Compound Interest Calculation

Present value	$100,000.00
Interest rate	7.5%
Term (years)	1
Compounding periods per year	12

#	Starting	Ending	#	Starting	Ending
1	$100,000.00	$107,763.26	12	$556,338.51	$599,528.51
2	$127,763.26	$137,681.85	13	$619,528.51	$667,624.12
3	$157,681.85	$169,923.11	14	$687,624.12	$741,006.17
4	$189,923.11	$204,667.33	15	$761,006.17	$820,085.05
5	$224,667.33	$242,108.84	16	$840,085.05	$905,303.04
6	$262,108.84	$282,457.03	17	$925,303.04	$997,136.72
7	$302,457.03	$325,937.55	18	$1,017,136.72	$1,096,099.69
8	$345,937.55	$372,793.59	19	$1,116,099.69	$1,202,745.41
9	$392,793.59	$423,287.17	20	$1,222,745.41	$1,317,670.31
10	$443,287.17	$477,700.71	21	$1,337,670.31	$1,441,517.13
11	$497,700.71	$536,338.51	22	$1,461,517.13	$1,574,978.51

In this table above, you can see 22 years are shown where in year one, the starting amount is $100,000. The $20,000 is not added until the start of year two and is continually added for the remainder of the years shown. In this scenario, a total of $540,000 is contributed by you throughout the 22 years. This would include the $100,000 original cash saved plus $20,000 per year until year 22. Based on 7.5% interest gained each year, the total interest earned is $1,034,978.51. This is a good illustration of why it is important to invest. You can earn a lot of money in interest. By investing, you are making your money work for you.

The original ask was to save $59K per year for 22 years to hit $1.4 million by the retirement age of 60 years old. With good money management and proper investing, you would only need to contribute $20,000 per year consistently for roughly 20 years, and you would hit $1.5 million at the retirement age. This beats the target by $100,000. By increasing the yearly contribution from $20,000 to $30,000, you would hit $2.1 million by the end

of your 22nd year. This is assuming you receive a 7.5%
return on investment. This is very possible and nothing
too outrageous.

This exercise is just to show you the magic of compound
interest and why investing early is key to a successful early
retirement. The more you invest each year and the earlier
you start, the better you should do in the long run. This
can be overwhelming at first and I can understand that.
Start with the two retirement tables I've shown in the start
of this chapter to plan out your age information and
funding information for retirement. After this is set, work
on the compound interest calculations in excel. To further
simplify everything, remember a lot of this work will start
the day your debt is fully paid off. We must also
remember our goals are personal and specific to our
needs.

To further illustrate this point, there are three boxes
shown here. The debt removal phase, retirement building
phase, and retirement phase. The first portion of your
career will be spent in the debt removal phase. This
means removing all your mortgage, car loan, credit card,
and student loan debts. The second portion will be the
retirement building phase. Once your debt has been
completely removed, you are ready to start building your
cash for retirement. You may have already started this in
your debt removal phase with a 401(k) or similar
investments. The difference here is that you will no longer
have any debt in this second phase, so you are going to be
heavy on the investments here. The final phase is in the
retirement period where you no longer are working. At
this point, you are expected to have all your money saved
up as planned for retirement. You are also making sure

you are budgeting accordingly, so you do not run out of money.

DEBT REMOVAL PHASE	RETIREMENT BUILDING PHASE	RETIREMENT PHASE

In estimating required funds for your retirement, I would not include social security. According to the Social Security and Medicare Board of Trustees, social security will be depleted by 2034. Since I will not be retired by this time, I will most likely not see a cent of my social security money, even though I paid into it. Of course, I am not happy about this, but will not dwell on negative forces. I will use this energy to focus on things I can control, such as building my own retirement fund. For reference, the Social Security and Medicare Boards of Trustee information is in a report titled, *A summary of the 2018 annual reports.*

Another important factor to take into consideration is your children. When you are planning your life out, you will obviously want to take them into consideration. It is possible they are going to want to attend college. College is increasingly expensive and the responsible thing to do is save up for their college tuition. You could make them pay, but this would mean they'd need to take out student loans. This can be very strenuous on students and they should be focused on their academics. Even if you cannot afford paying their complete tuition, it may make sense to put forward at least some of their tuition. This would require them to take out a smaller loan, which would potentially mean less interest.

We need to make sure we are planning in advance for any big financial event, such as our children going to college. We could be 100% debt free and the moment our children go to college, we can find ourselves in upwards of $100,000 in debt for each child. At that point, we are starting the debt cycle all over again. This is not what we want to do. An ideal situation would be full scholarships for my children, but this is not easy to come by. There are various options you can look into to prepare financially for your children's college expenses such as a ***529 plan***. The 529 plan is a tax advantaged savings plan designed to encourage savings for future education costs, according to the U.S. Securities and Exchange Commission. This is worth looking into to see if it aligns with your goals.

When we think about retirement, we might think about relaxing on the beach, drinking Pina coladas, listening to Jimmy Buffett or some other vacation music, and at peace financially. The reality is, so few are able to truly experience a retirement like this because they are not financially stable when they hit retirement age. So many have to work longer than they expected with little hope of getting the retirement they feel they deserve. Retirement planning should not begin a few years prior to retirement. Retirement planning should begin as soon as you start your career early on. We need to allow as much time as possible, so we can research and put efforts towards the plan we created.

You need to define the age you want to retire and age you reach 0% debt. You will need to calculate how much money you need in retirement. You need to calculate how much money on average you should put away each year leading up to retirement. Refer back to the tables I've described earlier on in this chapter. Think about where you are going to save the retirement money. Will it be in a savings with very little interest, but less risk? Will it be in a mutual fund with more interest, but more risk? Or will it be somewhere else? A good target for ROI (return on investment) is 7.5%.

You will also have the option to pay a financial advisor to invest your money. A financial advisor will charge you money and I personally would not use one at this point in my life. I do my own research and invest where I think it makes most sense. I do not want to have a middle-man or woman taking even more of my money to do something I can do myself. Again, this is personal preference and based on your level of comfort. You may not be very comfortable investing your own money, so you'd go to a financial investor. This is completely up to you, but I will say they are usually a bit expensive. They are going to require you to pay them fees for their services (obviously). It is also not a guarantee that you will receive great returns on your investment. However, it is guaranteed that the financial investor will take their cut of your money.

I remember reading an article based on the topic of, whether or not you should pay a financial investor. The article spoke to the point that you should not pay someone to invest your money. Financial investors cannot tell the future, so you are just as likely to pick a good investment. I'm not sure if I completely agree with this but can see where the writer was coming from. I cannot remember the exact article title because I do read quite a bit. You can read about some of the best investors of all time such as Warren Buffett, Benjamin Graham, Seth Klarman, and Jim Cramer to name a few. You can try to invest like them to grow your money. We do need to manage our expectations.

Warren Buffett is a professional investor and has made a staggering amount of money in his career of investing. He is the Michael Jordan of investing. I do not foresee myself being as successful as Warren Buffett when it comes to investing. Similarly, I would never imagine myself being as good as Michael Jordan in basketball. I can dribble around the court and make a few shots, but will never be in the NBA, let alone be the greatest. I could never see myself generating billions of dollars from investing. I would never be able to get to the level of Warren Buffett who is one of the greatest investors of all time.

I am capable of investing and gaining a 7.5% ROI or better on average per year. I tend to stay away from the riskier investments and focus on stocks that will give me a nice dividend. This dividend just gets reinvested immediately to further grow my stock portfolio. I know I am not a professional investor like Warren Buffett, John Templeton, or Jessie Livermore. I will never be the Michael Jordan of investors. When people get into risky investment portfolios, they are exposing themselves to possible devastation. Some people are able to handle the stress and potential loss. I personally am not willing to put my family's future at stake because the reward is not worth the risk in my opinion. I am satisfied with generating over $7,500 return per year for every $100,000 I have invested. Eventually, at $1 million invested you are expected to bring in over $75,000 return per year. This quickly adds up, but you need a 'big picture' mindset to see it.

Remember, my methods of reaching financial stability may not be your cup of tea. There are many ways to reach financial stability and mine may not be suitable for you. One key takeaway I hope you do remember is that we are accountable for our actions. We are responsible for our financial situation yesterday, today, and tomorrow. Retirement is quickly creeping up on us, if it didn't already, and we are responsible for making sure we are financially comfortable. Like illness and disease, you can take steps to prevent them, but may not have complete control over them. If you are going to develop a genetic disorder, it may happen regardless of what preventive measures you take.

Similar to illness, financial stability requires you to take certain steps, but these steps may not guarantee your success due to other outside factors. It is in our best interest to push hard on stabilizing our finances as early as possible to reduce the time we spend outside of financial stability. If we carry debt for 30 or 40 years, we are at risk for financial ruin for quite a bit of time. If we rid ourselves of debt in 15 years, we are removing 15 to 25 years of elevated financial risk. It is possible we lose our job at some point. It would be less severe to lose our job at a financially stable state versus a financially unstable state.

To be clear, I am not telling you to live your entire life dry without joys of purchasing things you'd like to have. I am simply saying plan your retirement out and restrict yourself from going too crazy on purchasing frivolous things you do not need. From time to time, it is okay to spend your money on yourself or your family. After all, we need to enjoy the present day. However, we do need to keep in mind we have a goal of retiring comfortably. If we determine our debt will be completely paid off by the age of 40 and need to put aside $30,000 each year for 25 years, then we need to stick to the plan. By missing these yearly targets, we are only hurting ourselves in the long-run. It is our responsibility to create the goal, plan to reach the goal, and execute the plan.

I fear being left behind and abandoned. I fear not being as valuable as my friends and family. If all my friends are retired at a comfortable age and I am still working hard, I'd be disappointed. I may also be a bit jealous because I did not have the option retire at the same age as my friends. I would not want to be in the office working while my friends are in the Bahamas drinking *Bahama Mamas* and *Pineapple Upside Down Martinis.* I would love to be a long side with my friends talking about the past and all the fun we had together. I'd also want to have the ability to take my children and their children on a vacation somewhere, without financial worries. These are the types of things I think about frequently that keep me motivated. These are very realistic goals and I am confident I can make them happen. Retirement should be enjoyable and can be. We just need to make sure we are planning for it.

I cannot remember when I first started using the term *financial stability*. When we do talk about financial stability, we are referring to a system that is resistant to economic shock. An example of economic shock would be losing your job unexpectedly due to the effects of a poor economy, which would lead to a period of time without income. If you are living paycheck to paycheck, unemployment can be detrimental to your financial situation. So, how do we prevent economic shock from turning our lives upside down? How can we prepare for an unexpected event occurring and creating financial hardship?

The best prevention of severe damage to our finances due to an unexpected circumstance is to build financial stability. We will want to determine what financial stability looks like, which is a personal estimate. Financial stability for someone living in Beverly Hills, California may be very different from financial stability for someone who lives in Montevallo, Alabama. The cost of living in Beverly Hills will be much higher than the cost of living in Montevallo. This would mean your annual operating cost would be much higher in Beverly Hills. Food, mortgage, rent, property tax, utility bills, insurance, and so on will all be much higher in Beverly Hills than Montevallo.

To understand our financial stability targets, we need to understand our current situation. First, we will want to know our annual operating costs to live our current lifestyle. This includes every expense we pay during the normal course of a year. The second piece of information is the length of time required to find a new job, if anything did happen. By multiplying the annual operating cost by years without a job, we get total funds required for financial stability. As an example, if our annual operating expense is $50,000 and we want two years to find a new job, our total funds required is $100,000. I would not expect it to take a full two years to find a job. It may only take 6 months, which would then require you to have $25,000 saved away. This would be the minimum and as always, we'd try to aim higher.

The issue with not having a job for a period of time is that you are not contributing to your 401(k) or other investments during that time. This is lost time that you are not going to get back where you could have been generating extra money for your financial stability. I struggle with this because we have limited time in life. If we start working at 20-years old and work until we hit 60-years old, we only have 40 solid years to work.

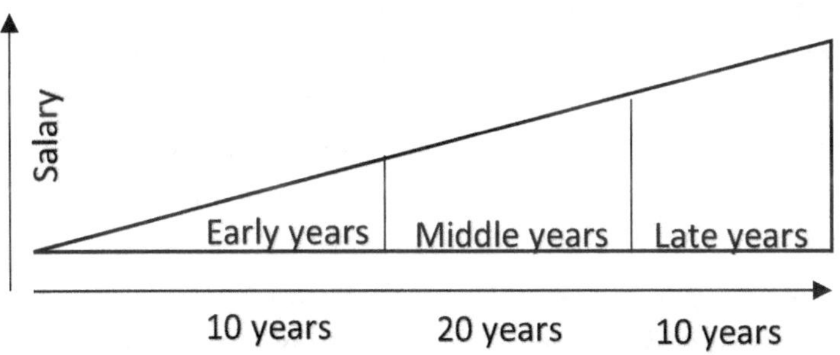

If I had to lay out the 40 years, I'd split it up as shown above. The early years would last about 10 years, middle years about 20 years, and late years about 10 years. During the early years, you are making the least amount of money because you have little experience. For most of us, our careers start immediately after college. It is also during this time that we are accruing the most interest from debts. Our loans will be the largest, which means the APR charge is going to also be the highest per year. It is not until you start lowering your debt that you will see your interest decrease per year.

I started my career as a chemist for a startup pharmaceutical company. I was not making much money at all and had some student loans to pay off. It was during my 5th year in my career as a packaging engineer when my fiancé and I purchased a home. This significantly increased our debt, so I was paying much more interest at the time. Keep in mind, I was in my first 10 years of my career, which I still deem as the early years in my career. I am not making a ton of money, yet my debt is the highest it will be throughout my career. I am getting hit with big interest and feel tight on funds.

The early years can be tricky because you are going to have temptation to spend money, since you probably went for so long without having much money in college. Most people leave college and get a little bit crazy in the first year or so, shopping for items they couldn't have before. They give into the urge of spending money and end up getting into debt. If you can manage this urge in your early years, you are winning half the battle. Again, we are usually not taught how to manage money in school unless you are majoring in a career that handles money, such as accounting, economics, or finance. As teachers, scientists, engineers, and most other careers, we are taught how to do our job. We are not taught how to manage money.

If we think about professional athletes, they are a great example of how things can go wrong if you don't manage your money well. There is Evander Holyfield, Mike Tyson, Allen Iverson, and Scottie Pippen to name a few. These athletes made a lot of money during their days as a professional athlete, but they did not manage their funds well. There was a time when these athletes lost a great deal of their fortune because they did not fight the urge to spend. Even though they were great at what they did in the ring or on the court, they were no Warren Buffett when it came to money management. There is something fundamentally wrong with athletes who earn extreme amounts of money and lose it all. This type of thing should never happen.

When a kid grows up poor and then gets signed to a professional sports team for a few million dollars, it enables the kid to buy almost anything they want. Additionally, this athlete is now hanging around with other athletes who are also making a lot of money and also spending it quickly. There may also be a level of competition between players to see who has the biggest house, most expensive cars, and grandest vacations. They may also have pressures from their family. Friends and family come out of the woodwork to receive handouts from the professional athlete. After the vacations, cars, houses, and handouts, the athlete doesn't have much left for himself and his future.

An athlete may believe they have a lot of time ahead of them to make more money. This does not always happen because teams cut players, players get injuries, and many other unexpected events can occur that stops the flow of money. Buying a large house, spending too much at a nightclub, and purchasing a Ferrari does not assure them financial stability. Most of us will not need to worry about this dilemma, which does not follow the normal career progression. There are no early years, middle years, late years progression with athletes. Usually, there is just the early years where they are making a lot of money and by the time they hit their tenth year, most are not making as much. So, we will not go further into this. If you are a big time athlete, you can personally call me and I can give you personal advice.

As we get into the middle years of our career, which spans roughly 20 years, we are making more money. Our responsibility should also go up and that is why we are getting paid more. We may need to manage more people, bigger accounts, or be expected to be more visible in the organization. We are getting paid more because we have more experience and are able to make effective decisions that will be more impactful to the business. If you are in your early years of your career, you should keep this in mind. We should always think about the next steps or next roles. Thinking about the next role isn't enough. We need to think two or three roles ahead to make sure we are getting what we need in our current role, to be successful in the next couple of roles.

As a packaging engineer, I would work on projects. The managers in packaging would think strategically, where I was more tactical. Since I knew the managers need a strategic mindset, I'd think about my own projects and try to think what I'd do if I was at the level of a manager. I'd try and ask the right questions and make sure what I was doing was right for the company in the short-term and long-term. If I did not think about the next role, I would not push myself to start learning about strategy and team management. I would remain stagnant or when I was given the opportunity to be a manager, I'd struggle.

When thinking back to the way I functioned in high school and partially in college, I could see I was very different as a professional. As I progressed through my early years in my career and then middle years, I could see an evolution of myself and the way I worked. I do not like to mention it much, but as we age, we can lose some strengths. Specifically, motivation can decrease if we continue on the same cycle with no changes. As humans it is natural to feel less driven when we are not seeing results when we are doing the same thing over and over again. This is not something we want to get stuck in. An endless loop of hard work and no results.

In the early years, managers should make sure you are not stuck in this endless loop of no hope. It is their job to guide you and make sure you are successful. With more experience, you can learn from your managers and mentors. You will be able to be more effective in producing results and need less guidance. In the early years, you are going to ask a lot of questions because it is part of the learning process. As you progress towards the end of the early years and into the middle years, you are going to transition into more of a leadership role. Others are going to look for your guidance, which is what you want. This does not mean, you are never going to have questions. It just means, more people will trust your judgment and knowledge.

The late years are when you are going to generate the most money and should last roughly 10 years. An external speaker spoke to my team years ago about this type of career progression. He referred to the late years as the harvest years because you are harvesting the bulk of your money in those years. To illustrate this point, I've created a table with average salaries for each phase of your career and the total amount earned during each phase.

Phase	Avg Salary	Total Earned	% of total earned
Early years (10 yrs)	$50,000	$500,000	15%
Middle years (20 yrs)	$80,000	$1,600,000	47%
Late years (10 yrs)	$130,000	$1,300,000	38%

If we follow the trend that is supposed to happen during your career, you should be earning more money as you progress forward. In the first 10 years, the average salary in this example is $50,000. If we multiply this by 10 years, we show that we earned a total of $500,000 during the early years phase. We can do this for the middle years and late years too. The first 10 years of our career, our earnings are much less than the middle years and late years. The middle years make up $1.6 million and the late years make up $1.3 million of our total earnings for our careers.

The early years make up 15% of the total salary earned in our 40 year career. We can compare this to the late years that make up 38% of the total earned. Both the early years and late years each take up 10 years of our career. For an apples to apples comparison, if we divide the middle years percentage of 47% by 2, we get 23.5%. We would divide this to normalize to 10 years, similar to the time period of the early years and late years. Either way, we are seeing that we are earning much more during the last 10 years of our career versus the first 10 years. Keep in mind this does not automatically happen and you need to work your way up to this phase. There are people that are making just as much or even sometimes less than when they first started in their late years.

There is a tool I use to help me understand how well I'm doing in terms of money-in and money-out. Similar to running a factory, I am looking for efficiencies in my finances to help stretch my money. A factory that is manufacturing cars is looking to see how fast they can push cars out to the consumer. If their capacity per day is 100 cars, but they are only completing 75 cars per day, they are only 75% efficient. A continuous improvement team would start looking around to see where their bottle neck is and would create a plan to increase efficiencies. Since I have a diverse background including engineering, I think about finances a little bit differently. I use efficiency as a KPI.

For those who are not familiar with KPI or key performance indicator, they are measurements used to drive continuous improvement. In the world of manufacturing, KPIs could be capacity utilization, customer complaints, asset utilization, efficiency, and so on. In the world of finance, KPIs could be profit, operational cash flow, inventory turnover, EBIT, and so on. When determining KPIs, you need to consider your goals and what is critical to achieving those goals.

In determining financial efficiency, you need to consider your total capacity or annual income. For this example, we will make $100,000 per year to keep the numbers simple. After tax, we are going to have $65,000 left for the year. I am using 35% tax for state and federal because I like to overestimate on tax rather than underestimate. The fourth row in the table is called Δfrom last year or change from last year. The number in the second column is $10,000. If you take a look back at chapter 5 – small gains, I go over a money tracker table to help track total saved, total debt, and actual money I have. This 'Δfrom last year' is calculated from the 'actual money I have' section of the tracker. You would subtract your December results from your January results in the same year to get the 'Δfrom last year' number.

Tracking	Amt ($)
Salary (before tax)	$100,000.00
Salary (after tax)	$65,000.00
Δfrom last year	$10,000.00
%efficiency	15%

By dividing 'salary (after tax)' by 'Δfrom last year' and multiplying by 100%, you gain your % efficiency of 15%. I would recommend using salary (after tax) rather than salary (before tax) because the tax is the tax. You are going to have to pay the tax no matter what and in my opinion is not controllable. There are things you can do to reduce the amount you need to pay for tax, but we should be doing this from the start anyways.

The 'actual money I have' figure is determined from the 'total saved' category and 'total debt' category that you should be tracking. 'Actual money I have' = 'total saved' – 'total debt'. In the early stage of your career, you will most likely be in the negatives. As you progress through your career closer to the middle years of your career, you are going to most likely be out of the negatives and into the positives, if you manage your money well.

The % efficiency figure is an important KPI because it tells you how well you are managing your money. This can be calculated on a monthly, quarterly, or yearly basis. I typically calculate it every year, but you may want to see it more frequently, depending on what you are looking for. Your salary (after tax) is considered your total capacity or the amount of money you have before any expenses occur. Any sort of expense such as insurance, utilities, gas for your car, maintenance for your car, and so on, will decrease your % efficiency. Nonvalue expenses such as interest, fees, and charges will also decrease your % efficiency. It is our job to recognize the areas where we can improve. We will want to get all nonvalue add expenses out.

A nonvalue expense is interest, which is why we need to remove all debt as quickly as we can. If you have a mortgage for $200,000 at a 5% APR, you are spending roughly $10,000 in interest per year. By removing this mortgage and keeping everything else the same, you are now at 31% efficiency. Our goal is to continuously push up the % efficiency KPI each year. Our goal is also to increase our salary each year. By consistently improving these two figures alone, we are going to be in much better shape several years out.

Tracking	Amt ($)
Salary (before tax)	$100,000.00
Salary (after tax)	$65,000.00
Δfrom last year	$20,000.00
%efficiency	31%

It's important to track and trend your financial portfolio. The better you get to know it, the more likely you are going to be able to make better decisions. A good

%efficiency range is 60 to 75%. If you can get higher than this, then you should do it. Keep in mind the different phases of your career that we discussed earlier on in this chapter. The early years, middle years, and late years of your career have different financial properties in terms of salary, debt, and investments. In other words, our financial stability will vary at each phase of our career. Our financial stability will vary at each phase of our life.

In our early years, we are expected to be less stable because we do not have a strong financial foundation. We are working to build this foundation during the first 10 years of our career. Our middle years are where we are more established and working towards saving for our retirement. There are some who say we should not worry about retirement until much later, but we can never be too sure what the future holds. Will we be healthy enough to continue working in our late years? Will an unexpected tragic event occur that turns our lives upside down? The sooner we can reach financial stability, the better.

Years ago, when my wife and I were meeting with our pastor and his wife for marriage counseling, we were told a story that changed my thoughts on preparation for the future. The marriage counseling was required before getting married by my church. During a session of marriage counseling, our pastor and his wife told us a story about themselves right after they were married. It was a story about life and unexpected changes. The message was about how things can change quickly and we need to be prepared for them. We also need to stick together no matter what.

My wife and I have always stuck together, even if we did experience a difficult time. We have always told ourselves that we would always work things out as a team. Our pastor and his wife told us about their first real challenge right after being married. During this time in their life, they were doing pretty good financially and had big plans for the future, but then a life changing moment happened. The pastor and his wife were in a terrible car accident that prohibited them from working. The inability of working and large medical bills nearly crippled them financially. They quickly realized they would not be able to live the way they dreamed about. They also quickly realized material things were not the most important thing in life.

I completely agree with the pastor and his wife. Material things are not the most important things in life. However, money is a universal language and helps you live a little bit easier. Money can get you things to help you enjoy life a little bit more and perhaps, not have as tough of a time in some situations. For example, most colleges can be pretty expensive. If my son one day wants to go to a prestigious school and is accepted, then it is my duty to make sure I have the money to get him in there. I do not want money to limit my sons on what they can and cannot do. I want to allow them every opportunity possible. This is my duty as a father.

Financial stability is a personal preference in most cases, which is why it is important for you to figure out what financial stability means to you. Does it mean having a few dollars in the bank in case you lose your job? Or does it mean, having a few million dollars in the bank, so you can go out and really enjoy your retirement? Whatever you land on, you should have some sort of justification in your assessment.

We are not very financially stable during the early years in our career. This is our most vulnerable time in our life when it comes to money. For most of us, we are bringing on large debt and making the least amount of money, relative to our career path. During this time, you may have the expense of a wedding and have a few children, which can also be expensive. In particular, weddings can be very expensive, and this can be an expense that is not easy to avoid. It ties into our emotions and would not make us feel good if we got cheap on this important day in our life. We want our wedding to be perfect and we can believe the more money we spend, the more perfect our wedding will be. I can say confidently, this is not true. The more you spend on a wedding does not mean you will have a happier marriage than someone who spent less on their wedding.

It was during my early years when I paid for my own wedding. This was my choice for the most part. I did not want to burden anyone else with the large cost of a wedding. I also wanted my wife and I to have full control of who we invited and what the wedding looked like. If we had someone else help us out or pay for it completely, we would most likely have less control of the wedding. I did not want to deal with that situation. By asking someone else to chip in on our wedding, we could have introduced more stress. We did not want to add more stress or opportunity for family feuds. We wanted everyone to feel at ease and just enjoy themselves. My wife and I would be fully responsible for providing a good time to our guests.

It was also during my early years when my wife and I had two sons. This also increased our expenses significantly, but we did manage the best we could. Daycare is an expensive service, which can cost you upwards of $1,500 per month. After touring a few daycare centers, my wife and I decided it was best if she stayed home with our kids. She ended up picking up some night shifts and shifts on the weekends. This is something she could do in the medical field. This was not an option I had for my career.

Our mortgage was a very large undertaken in our early years, but I felt it was necessary. I did not want to rent an apartment where 100% of that rent would not go towards a future investment, such as my own house. At the same time as this, my wife and I both had car payments, which we were paying off as quickly as possible. My wife and I also both had student loans during our early years in our career.

As you can see, I had a lot of debt during my early years in my career. Looking back, it was slightly frightening to think about how much debt we had. And to think, I consider myself pretty good with money. I do not think there was any way around the debt we did acquire. We needed cars to get to our workplace and back. We needed a place to live. We needed schooling to get into our careers. All this debt was essential in my opinion. I also believe it was essential to get the debt removed as quickly as possible, to minimize the interest that was eating away at our financial momentum forward.

There is a lot to think about when it comes to financial stability. At this point, I believe you should have the tools to begin creating goals and planning steps to reach those goals. In some form, financial stability should be one of our goals. We may not specifically say financial stability. We may refer to it as retirement or adequate funding to support any unpredictable event that comes our way. We all know financial stability is important even if we do not want to admit it. This is not something that typically occurs by itself and we need to be intentional. We need to make sure we are concentrating on it each month by tracking our numbers and looking for continuous improvement. We need to keep financial stability top of mind.

I never thought I'd be a packaging engineer or in supply chain. At one point, I never thought I'd work as a chemist or have a business manufacturing equipment. In my youth, I had dreams of being in a rock band touring the world. I also had dreams of playing in the National Hockey League for the Detroit Red Wings. I wanted to pitch for the Cleveland Indians. I wanted to be an actor in Hollywood movies. I wanted to be a writer and my first book would have been, *The Adventures of Fez and Johnny Jingles*. The reality is, most of us will never be what we wanted to be when we were younger. This is not necessarily a bad thing. We cannot all live in a Hollywood movie where the ending is magical. However, we can still live a happy ending if we plan appropriately.

I realized I was not going to play for the Red Wings or Cleveland Indians during my junior year in high school. I realized I was not going to be a Hollywood movie actor or in a famous band around the same time. I spent quite a bit of time stocking shelves at the local Shop Rite in Hammonton, New Jersey during my last two years of high school. They would give me 39 hours per week to keep me part time and would not need to provide me benefits. The full-time employees did receive benefits and were making much more than me.   My hourly rate was $6, so even with 39 hours per week, I was only making $234 per week. Then you would have to deduct taxes, union dues, social security, and so on.

Thinking back on my days at Shop Rite, it is absolutely crazy how little I was making. I worked in the dairy department, so I was responsible for making sure all the inventory was rotated regularly. Products for the dairy department were delivered every two days and I was responsible for getting all those products on the shelf before the next shipment came in. The dairy manager and other dairy workers were lazy, so I was expected to do a lot of the heavy lifting. They would act like they worked all day, but I knew they could not have possibly worked much at all. I started my shift around 3pm on the weekdays and 8am on the weekends. Eventually I caught on and realized I was the only one really working in the dairy department. I realized they left everything for me.

During my first few weeks on the job, my manager took me aside and told me I was not moving fast enough. He told me if I could not keep up, I would not have a job at Shop Rite. This scared me, especially because this was my first real job working for an employer. I pushed myself to be the best I could be. I'd clock out for my mandatory breaks and go back to work. I did not want to disappoint my manager or the other team members. Looking back, I now know he was a little bit of a bully and wanted me to pick up his slack. It was later on when I learned he would sit in his office eating donuts all day because he knew I'd finish his work. The only one being a team player was me. My manager and other co-workers in dairy were not team players and this is a lesson I'd remember for the rest of my life. A manager who wants to be respected by his employees should contribute to the team's efforts in some way. He should not hold himself above everyone else.

At one point later on in my career at Shop Rite, I sliced my leg open with a box cutter. The knife cut through my pants and into the side of my leg. Since the blade was so sharp, I did not realize I was cut until I felt the blood dripping down my leg. It felt cold and wet. A co-worker of mine named Will who looked exactly like the rapper T.I. took me to the bathroom to look at my leg. The skin was flapping in the wind and blood was everywhere. I told my manager on the way out that I needed to seek medical attention. My manager told me not to leave without clocking out first. The clock was located all the way in the back of the store, so I had to end up walking back through the store with my leg bleeding everywhere. I can still remember the feeling of the blood dripping down my leg inside of my pants. I can still remember the stickiness of the blood as it contacted the interior of my pants.

As you can see, this was not the best place to work because my manager was not the nicest of people. I also was only making $6 per hour, which is not a livable wage today. Even with inflation, this dollar amount today would be roughly $8 and that would still not be livable. Luckily, I did not need money back then for anything, but gas for my car and entertainment with friends. However, I knew I could not live on this wage for the rest of my life. From the year or so of working at Shop Rite, I did not save much money at all. The experience of dealing with customers was a very important lesson for me. There were days when I'd have incredibly nice customers and other days when the customers were toxic. For the most part, the customers were enjoyable to talk with.

After high school, I ended up leaving Shop Rite and going to UMDNJ-SOM as an assistant for one of their specialty departments. In the department, there were many psychologists and medical doctors. This provided me with the opportunity to seek advice from knowledgeable professionals. I was going to the local community college for psychology during this time. Many of the psychologists who had their PhD or PsyD told me not to pursue the field of psychology. They claimed their salary was not what they thought it would be. They were also dealing with some depressing cases, which often led them to have their own psychologists. The environment and type of people who worked for UMDNJ-SOM were outstanding. These were the type of professionals I wanted to work with. Even if I did not pursue psychology as a career, I would still want to work in a similar environment with similar people. This environment was very different from Shop Rite.

After I went to a 4-year college away from home, I could no longer work for UMDNJ-SOM. This was roughly around the time when my father and I started our own business. This was also roughly around the time I met my friend in school named Sendhur Gautham who pushed me into switching from psychology to biochemistry. This change led me to my first real job as a chemist for a startup pharmaceutical company. Although, this company did not pay well, gave no benefits, and working conditions were poor, I learned a significant amount. I'd say I learned much more from this experience than if I went to a larger corporation because I was given the freedom to work on everything.

After 3-years as a chemist, I went to maintenance, then packaging, and then supply chain. At each step of the way I've worked to gain as much knowledge as possible and network with everyone I could. It does not matter if someone is a janitor, vice president, group manager, engineer, or operations manager. Each person you network with is going to teach you something, which could potentially be key to your future success. I will say, do not connect with someone just because you think they are going to give you something or be beneficial to you in some way. Think about how you can also give them something too. Nobody likes a 'user'.

During my time in packaging, I had two mentors. One was a technical mentor to help me further grow my technical expertise. The second mentor was someone who could help me further grow my knowledge of the business world. The technical stuff was something I was dealing with day to day. The business stuff was not something I was dealing with day to day. He was a business operations manager named Justin. He was the first person to mention succession planning to me. He gave me a sneak peak of supply chain's succession plan. I realized packaging did not have a succession plan, which made me think career development in packaging was not as good as supply chain. This was evident when you looked at the past couple of years and the lack of career movement within the department.

My mentor Justin also spoke to me about effective presenting because this was an area I was interested in improving. He also helped me setup meetings with various people in supply chain that were in different roles. Some of these roles were demand planning, supply planning, capacity planning, co-manufacturer managers, quality, logistics, and so on. He made me aware that if I wanted to get into supply chain or any other department, that I should figure out the different roles in that department to see where I fit best. Sounds pretty simple, but I was not fully aware of this during this time. Even just meeting with these different roles, gave others awareness of who I was and that I was looking.

If others are not aware that you want better opportunities, then they may not offer you these opportunities. It is important to make sure our managers are aware that we want more responsibility and more opportunities to grow. Each day you are working, you are showing the leadership team you are capable of greatness. It's important to dress nicely every day and look your best. You never know when you are going to be pulled into a meeting with important people. There have been plenty of incidences where this happened to me. There have been times when I felt underdressed because I did not plan for a meeting with leadership. There have been times I was dressed nicely and was relieved when I was pulled into the meeting with leadership.

As silly as it sounds, looking good is very important. It is important to make sure you look good all the time. This means keeping a healthy look and often that means, exercising and eating healthy regularly. Make sure you smell clean and have clean clothes on. Make sure those clothes are fitting for the occasion. All of these things will help you feel more confident. Whenever I feel I look bad, it irks me. It is one more thing I have lingering in the back of my mind that does not allow me to move on. When I dress nice, feel fit, and have a clear mind, I feel more confident and ready for my day. On the days I feel great about myself, it takes much more to knock me down, metaphorically speaking.

During one of my business trips down to Dallas, I had the opportunity to sit next to the Senior Vice President of

Supply Chain. At the Philadelphia International Airport I spotted him waiting to board the same airplane as me. I had no intention of seeing him that day and have never met him before. At first, I wanted to introduce myself, but I became nervous. I told myself if I sat near him, I would make an attempt to introduce myself. By chance he was sitting across the aisle from me in seat 12D. My seat was 12C. I had my notebook sitting on my lap with my company's name on it, which was the same company he worked for. He looked over and asked me if I worked for that company. I said yes and introduced myself. He introduced himself and I responded, *I know who you are. I did not want to bother you.*

The SVP of Supply Chain and I talked for a good portion of the flight from Philadelphia to Dallas. He told me to setup a meeting with him when I returned to the office. I did take this opportunity because it is not an opportunity everyone gets. I ended up talking with him in his office weeks later and the conversation was pretty good. Still till this day he knows who I am, and it is all because I met him on an airplane from Philadelphia to Dallas. Fortunately, I was dressed nicely the day of the flight. I always think back to that day and know if I was not dressed nicely, I would have avoided contact with him at all costs. Anytime I am going out to fly somewhere, I think twice about what I'm going to wear. I always meet random people on flights. You never know when one of those people will be a future opportunity or your SVP of Supply Chain.

Career development or career building is incredibly important to our success in life, or at least for me it is. If you do not care about your career and want to produce minimal results if that, then this book may not be for you.

Similar to the way we use small gains in building your financial portfolio, small gains also applies to career development. We do not necessarily need to make huge leaps from one role to another role. We do not need to become CEO overnight. In fact, we do not need to become CEO ever to be successful. Your goals are personal and should be custom to your lifestyle.

I made some unique moves in my career from chemist to maintenance and from maintenance to packaging engineer. Then I went from packaging engineer to supply quality. Advice from a few professionals I spoke with was, think about not only the next role you want, but the next two roles you want. Work through the skillsets and talents you need to get each one of those roles. You may also want to think about some other roles that would be alternatives in case you decide one day you do not want to pursue the original desired role. We need to make sure we are constantly setting ourselves up for success. We want to make sure we are not randomly closing doors for no good reason.

To understand what you need to get for each role, you should meet with the manager you would report to or someone that knows the role. It could be someone who works in that role, has worked in that role, or someone who works with the role closely. Understand expectations of the role and skillsets you need to build prior to being able to take on the role. A lot of this does require you to live outside of your comfort zone. In most cases, you do not need to learn everything overnight. The sooner you identify the role or roles you would like to be in, the sooner you can start building your skillset for the identified role. Since you will have time, you can make small gains to build your skillset. Ideally, you will want to have more time than what is necessary to achieve what you need. On the flip side, you do not want to push out your promotion or transition to another role too far because this would further delay your career development.

There are various paths you can take to build the skillsets you need for another role. The most popular way is experience. You can work on projects that will help you build specific skills for the role you identified. You can gain some experience from shadowing. I would say although shadowing is beneficial, most don't truly learn how to do something until they've tried it for themselves. My process of learning typically begins with observation and then participation. First, I observe how someone else does it. Then I try it myself with supervision. Once I feel comfortable enough, I will perform the task without supervision. It can be challenging to take lead because we can get nervous. I have always found that when I take lead, my nervousness quickly leaves me. The anticipation itself can really hold people back from living their dreams.

Another path to build skillsets is school or continued education. There are times when an employer requires you to have a certain level of education. Even if you feel you have the skillsets necessary to be successful in that role, the employer may still require a piece of paper as part of your credentials. This can be frustrating, but at times there may not be any way around it. I've known people who were fully qualified for the job and did not receive the job, solely because they did not have the degree they needed. I believe you are never too old to learn. We should never stop learning. If a piece of paper is the only thing between us and the job we want, we better find a way to get that piece of paper. There may be no way around it.

I know people who thought about going to school in their early twenties. They thought about it quite a bit, but never did enroll. They reached their thirties and still did not have their degree. In that ten years, they could have finished school and worked for several years building experience. This creates a feeling of anxiety and can make someone feel trapped. The longer they go without correcting their error of not enrolling in school, the less likely they will enroll later on. This can be a vicious cycle and I'd wish this on nobody. We all need to be proactive and do things when the opportunity presents itself. Even if you didn't get to school when you should have, it is never too late. Start today by enrolling because in a few years, you will be grateful you did.

Career building is important because it makes you more valuable and marketable. You are your own brand and need to build your brand. Each day, you are contributing to your brand. How do you want people to see you? This is extremely important in career building because so much depends on it. Opportunities may or may not be given to you based on your brand. Imagine a role opens up in your company, which would be a promotion for you. This is a serious role where you would need to interact with leadership. You decide to apply for the job and the hiring manager reviews your resume. You have all the requirements needed for the job, so you are qualified, right?

Imagine the hiring manager now asks around the office who you are. The hiring manager is told you are somewhat of a clown and not serious. They say you get your work done but like to joke around. The hiring manager immediately eliminates you from the running because they are looking for someone serious. Your brand is jokester, when the desired role requires someone who is serious. This would be a major problem. Most likely, you may never know why you did not get the opportunity. Even if you did get a courtesy interview, the hiring manager will already have preconceived opinions about you. Think of the countless ways your brand can be misrepresented and prevent you from acquiring an opportunity.

I bring this example up because I've had my own experiences with misconstrued branding. When I first joined the packaging department, I was somewhat immature. I took on a professional position, yet nobody ever taught me how to be professional. I was not immature to a point where I could have lost my job. I still did good work. I still got everything done that I needed. I did my best to go above and beyond. I was known to joke around a lot in the office, as if I was trying to win a popularity contest. After the first year or so, I tried to change my style in the office. At this point, it was too late, and everyone still thought of me as a jokester. I tried being more serious, but my brand was ingrained in everyone's mind.

For the remainder of my time in packaging, I was not taken too seriously. I ended up moving into supply chain where I could build a new brand for myself. I did just that because I wanted to be taken seriously and have opportunities to move into larger roles. I was successful in building my new brand but did feel it was easy to revert to my old ways. I'd have to constantly remind myself that I was now serious. I had plenty of time to joke around and be immature at home with my family and friends. There may be times you want to build a brand where you are looked at as the funny guy or girl. For me and the culture of the company I worked for, the brand needed to be serious. People equate seriousness with someone who will get results, no matter what. This is exactly how I wanted my co-workers and managers to see me. I wanted to be seen as someone who gets results.

The outcome of building a serious brand for myself did produce me the results I was looking for. I ended up gaining more respect from my co-workers and managers. Fewer people would try stepping on me. I was no longer just the nice guy in the office. I was now somebody who had an opinion that mattered. I was also offered more opportunities and roles in various functions. The rebranding of myself was not something that happened overnight. However, it was something that was worth the effort. Your brand should make sense for what you want to be and where you want to go. How do you want people to see you? What do you want people to take away after meeting you? What is most important to you and your brand? These are questions you need to think about when building your personal brand.

In our careers, there are three main areas we need to look at. These areas are – location, salary, and role (in no particular order). The level of importance for each is a personal preference. Even if we are satisfied with our current role and company, we should keep our eyes open for other opportunities. There may be another opportunity that provides you with a better place to live, more money, or better role. I think we can all agree it is much easier today to find new opportunities than it was many years ago. The internet provides endless results for careers across the World. You can even find salary estimates for jobs at various companies in various locations. We have no excuse not to investigate other opportunities. I would also say because it is easier to find out which opportunities are good ones, there will be more people applying for the better opportunities. This could make it much more competitive to find a good job. It is up to you to position yourself in such a way, where you are the best candidate for the job.

As much as I'd love to say, stay loyal to your current employer, I also know employers are not always loyal to their employees. Specifically, public companies are going to do whatever it takes to give their shareholders value. Especially today, cost cutting is a very popular way to provide value to the shareholder. When sales are not growing as quickly as the company would like, cutting out the bottom line is the next best thing. Cost cutting can be materials savings, energy savings, or labor savings to name just a few. When the company is not doing well, there is almost always labor reduction. I can understand this because the thinking is, not one employee is more important than the entire company. When I say this, I am talking in terms of financials and not safety.

I have personally felt stuck in a role with no movement. I've seen others in a similar situation and did not do anything about it. I am not the type to sit around and wait for a miracle. I will always manage my own career because I know managers do not always go out of their way to help you grow in your career. There have been times I've had a manager intentionally hold me back because they did not want to put in the effort to promote me. There would always be that one reason they did not promote me. They would dangle the carrot in front of me to keep me working, but I'd never get the carrot. Instead of chasing the unreachable carrot, change your direction and get another carrot that is larger and taste better. This is what I've done in my career multiple times and it always turned out great.

In this chapter, we talked about a wide variety of things that can help you grow in your career. A key takeaway is that you need to hold yourself accountable for your own career. Nobody is going to tap you on the shoulder and give you extra money. The thought is you are doing the job and not complaining, so why give you more money. It's not necessarily a bad thing to represent yourself as a flight risk. If you are valuable, your employer will want to keep you. Anytime an employer needs to replace an employee, it can cost them a significant amount of money. There is the money needed to recruit and train. There is the time where the new employee is not contributing value to the company. No company wants to replace an employee, especially when they are good.

Continue to build your brand to further the growth of your career. Your brand includes your look. Never show up to work looking poorly. As mentioned, you never know when you will have to meet with leadership or someone that can provide greater opportunities to you. You also do not want to be the type to gossip or cause drama in the workplace. This is a sure way to get into trouble. Make sure you keep political beliefs outside of work. Anything sensitive should be left outside of the workplace because this can cause issues.

There is also something else that has really helped me along the way and was something I learned later on in my career. Effectiveness is crucial to getting results in a timely manner. We have limited hours in a day and need to focus on the projects that contribute maximum benefit to the business. This requires us to have knowledge of the business and the direction the business wants to go. This also requires us to understand what our managers' objectives are for the year. We need to make sure we are focused on getting them to their objectives. Usually, our objectives are going to be subsets of their larger objectives.

I wish I could say career growth was exclusive of politics, but in most cases it is not. There are times when certain individuals are promoted or offered better opportunities because they are better politicians than you. Perhaps they have spent more time getting to know leadership than you have. Perhaps they are going to lunch with their managers and spending weekends over their houses. There are a multitude of approaches to building relationships with leaders in the organizations. My recommendation is to do the best job you can and try to stay connected with the decision makers in your organization. There is nothing wrong with building relationships with leadership. In fairness, I'd want to know my workers too.

Look at the scenario from the perspective of the leader. Most people rarely take this approach. Most will just complain that certain people in their organization are brown nosing and that is why they are getting the promotions. This may be true, but from the leader's perspective, they are promoting who they trust most. I too would want to be surrounded by people who I trust. I'm not going to promote someone who does good work, but I do not know personally. The person that does good work could also be a creep.

For many years, I never thought about the political matters in this way because I was taught it was not the right way. Similarly, I was taught competition was not the right way. I was taught to share and let others have what I wanted. When you have your own family, you need to do what is right for them. I remember a time when my father let a co-worker take a role he wanted because his co-worker seemingly wanted it more. His co-worker also had a young family and may have needed the money more. That sounds nice, but what about my father's family, meaning his wife and kids. My brother and I could have used some extra cash. I can remember a few times I was not given something because cash was tight. What about my father's family? My father should have taken the job and did what was right for his own family.

They also say the squeaky wheel gets the grease. If you are not squeaky, then you are not getting that grease. The grease can be money, promotion, new role, new opportunity, and so on. I can remember when I was younger playing baseball and was benched pretty much all season. I would play the standard 2 or 3 innings because it was the rule of the league. All kids had to play 2 or 3 innings per game. I wasn't bad at all. In fact, I was very good at baseball. The issue was I pitched and played 2nd base. These were the two positions the coach's son played. The coach would put his son in, and I'd be left to sit on the bench. The only innings I'd play were when the coach's son was pitching.

There was one game when we were down, and the bases were loaded. The coach's son was pitching and really doing poorly. The coach was embarrassed of his son, so he decided to put me in to pitch. He was probably thinking I'd do worse and make his son look slightly better. With bases loaded and no outs, I took the pitching mound. It was top of the lineup and odds were against me. I remembered everything my brother taught me. I struck the first out. My confidence was slightly higher. I struck the second out. My confidence was higher, and I was smiling. I struck the third out and my team was excited. I was smiling ear to ear. The coach's son was depressed on the bench. The coach came up to me and said I could work on a few things. The coach was not pleased with my performance because it further proved his son was not as good as me.

If I could go back in time, I would have been a squeaky wheel and demanded to pitch in the beginning of the season. This was one of the last games of the season and it was too late. It gave me a sour feeling because it was unfair how I could not play more. I also wished my father stood up to the coach and demanded that I play more. I really had a sour feeling inside when I was benched the first 3 innings of a game and the game ended early due to inclement weather. I decided not to talk to my parents for the rest of the night because of how upset I was. I was the only kid on the team who was benched and did not play that game. The coach said he would put me in the first inning the next game. I still can feel the anger and disappointment from that day. I will never let this happen to my children.

Some of the best advice I can give on career growth is not to be quiet and feel you have no control over your career. You are completely in control and fully accountable. Nobody else will give you the opportunities you can give yourself. Only you can set yourself up for success by successfully completing school, gaining experiences, and taking opportunities presented to you. You are responsible for building your brand, networking, and keeping your eye open for greater opportunities out there. They say if you are not growing, then you are dying. We do not want to die before we've lived. Using small gains every day we can reasonably grow and achieve great results overtime. Everyday counts when it comes to career growth. We must always remember this.

Have you ever thought about how you got from point A to point B? As we move forward in life, we are met with many opportunities and it is our job to decipher which are worth our time. Some of the choices we make in life can go well, while other times, not so well. As we go through some doors, other doors may open or close. We can resist opportunities and if we wait long enough, those opportunities will vanish. Opportunities are a function of time. They are dependent on our surroundings. From time to time, we may think it's luck or being at the right place at the right time. There seems to always be some uncertainty when we are determining if we should partake in opportunities. There are times we won't get all the facts and need to take risks.

Worse than making a poor decision, making no decision leaves your fate in the hands of others. The occasional opportunity in the workplace may come up. You may think about the opportunity for a while. It is imperative to make a decision on whether or not you are going to take it. By avoiding the decision and the people asking you the question, will do more harm than good. More importantly, I do not want to wait around for an answer due to someone else's lack of certainty. The point here is, we need to make decisions and make sure they are made quickly. We can miss out on opportunities if we do not jump in with speed.

Not too long ago, I had a manager who would talk about making big moves for our team. He would campaign his ideas in our team meetings to make sure his team knew he was working towards getting our team more attention. In doing this, I assumed other cross-functional partners also knew of our team's goals. In speaking to our cross-functional partners, I quickly found out this was not the case. In fact, I was the only one pushing on our focus objectives and influencing others to buy into them. We needed the buy in of other teams to accomplish our goals. My manager at the time was not communicating these objectives, nor putting much effort towards them. This became concerning to me because I felt my manager was not doing what he said he was doing.

One day, I went up to my manager and asked him if he had any status updates on our project. As always, he talked about the long process and many challenges to accomplish such a large goal. He was waiting on others to approve our process because they needed to participate in the process we created. I ended up asking my manager a few times about the status of the project. Each time, I received a similar response. This is when I became frustrated because the cross-functional partners I was working with didn't hear directly from my manager about this project. It felt as if, I was going crazy and telling these people lies. This put me in a difficult position because I now needed to deal with my manager. I now had to squeeze him for truthful answers and actions we would take to redirect our path forward.

Just because someone manages you, does not mean you cannot persuade them to be better. In fact, it is our job to make our managers better because our careers depend on it. I ended up giving my manager my own ideas on how we should work through the approvals. We started rolling out the process without full approval from all cross-functional teams. The beginning was a pilot of our new process. A few months went by and we began seeing good examples of wins we could share with our cross-functional partners. Leadership quickly realized our team did add value and they were appreciative of the improvements we made. The other cross-functional partners and approvers of the process had no choice, but to approve at this point. When leadership likes something, it is your job to push forward and make that something happen.

Decisions are crucial to getting to the next phase in your project or process. We need to decide if we are going to take on new opportunities or not. Letting tough decisions linger will not make it any easier. It could actually make your life more difficult. Imagine waiting a month to make a decision and that decision leads you to failure. This same decision could have been made in a week. You have now wasted three extra weeks. These extra weeks could have been used to regroup and correct your mistake. Getting extra time whenever and wherever you can, could make a big difference.

Another important factor in taking advantage of opportunities that can lead you to success is, diversification. Similar to investing your money, it is always good to diversify your career opportunities. Similarly, it is always good to have multiple streams of income. When we look at debt, we will always have multiple streams of money going out. We will have our taxes, utilities, grocery bills, and other expenses. There are always multiple expense streams. It is not a huge deal if we get rid of an expense stream. In fact, that is usually a good thing. If we only have one income stream, then if we lose it, we are in deep trouble.

To help our odds, we should try to have multiple streams of income. If you have a husband or wife, and they work, then you have two streams of income. Having a third or fourth stream of income is even better. The benefit of more streams of income is having more opportunities to generate money. A larger income will help you reduce debt faster and more quickly save for retirement. If you do lose a stream of income, you will have another stream or two to generate money and continue living. We do want to continue growing our income each year, especially knowing inflation is also growing at 3% to 4% each year.

Of course, there are down sides to having more streams of income. Each stream of income, in most cases, does require you to spend more time working. In planning our futures, we can take this into account. It is better to get all of our traveling and putting in our long hours prior to having a family. Family should always be your number one priority. Obviously, we need to financially support our family. We do need to make sure we are also supporting them emotionally too. Spending quality time with your family is extremely important.

My father missed much of my childhood due to working nonstop, but I cannot be too upset. He did this so my mother could be home full time with my brother and me. He did not want us to be watched by a stranger and I'm grateful for that. My father at 30 years old and myself at 30 years old, are in different situations. My father started from a lower class than myself. Through my father's efforts, he was able to elevate his family to a higher class. This allowed my brother and me to have a much better childhood than my father, from a financial perspective. I am not saying my father had a bad childhood. It was just different and I respect that.

I want to also elevate my children to a higher class than I was raised in. I am not saying middle class is unacceptable. I'd just like to see my children have endless opportunities and be as successful as possible. I want them to be happy and live prosperous lives. I'd want my children to do much better than myself. I will always be proud of them, no matter what. The range of opportunities one is introduced to can be limited by the wealth of their family. Limited resources can equate to one's inability to take certain paths. If I can get to a point where my financial situation is not a barrier to the opportunities my children get, then I would be very satisfied.

I have always kept two streams or more of income and believe this has helped tremendously. There are going to be times when you need some extra money. Your primary income may not be able to cover unexpected expenses. This could be your washing machine breaking, needing a new roof, or your car breaking. You should be saving some extra money for a rainy day, but there are times when this does not happen. Especially, during your early years, you are taking some more risks to get your debt paid down faster. During my early years, I was putting everything I had into getting my mortgage paid off. I did not want to keep paying thousands in interest each year, for every year it was not paid off.

Previously, I provided this table showing monthly income and expenses. As you continue to track your income and expenses over the years, you will start realizing trends. If you are managing your money correctly, you should start seeing your expenses decreasing year over year. You should also see your income increasing year over year. If this is not happening, then there is something wrong and you need to investigate. Since we are talking opportunities for success in this chapter, I am bringing this up for a very specific reason. As we get to know our financial situation better on a monthly and yearly basis, we will start to realize that we need to increase our income. Opportunities you did not think of for yourself in the past, may start making more sense now. You should also realize some of those higher paying jobs with more responsibilities, can be suitable for you. I believe getting to know your financial situation better will be fuel to motivate you to get uncomfortable and jump into things you wouldn't normally jump into.

	January	February
Savings	$1,000	1,200
Checking	$1,000	1,200
401K	$5,000	5,500
Total Saved	**$7,000**	**$7,900**
Electric	$100	$100
Gas	$100	$100
Credit Card	$200	$200
Cable / Internet	$100	$100
Cellular Phone	$100	$100
Water	$25	$25
Mortgage	$1,500	$1,500

Home insurance	$200	$200
Property Taxes	$200	$200
Car loan	$350	$350
Car insurance	$100	$100
Student loans	$500	$500
Total Debt	$3,675	$3,675
Actual Money I have	$3,325	$4,225

It can be devastating to find yourself falling behind on your bills. It can also be depressing to find yourself falling behind all your friends. You may start asking why some others are doing so much better than you. You probably don't really know how well they are doing, so it could be for show only, but that is besides the point. My reviewing of my monthly financial tracker helps me realize I do not need that new expensive car. It makes me think twice about going out and buying new clothes for myself. It also helps me prepare in advance for upcoming financial events.

We should also touch on how much you should save versus invest versus contribute to debt removal. A lot of people will say 10% for investment and 5% for savings. Others will say 10% for savings and no mention of investments. This is truly a personal preference and you should justify why you are saving, investing, and contributing to debt removal. Everyone's goals are going to be slightly different, so why should everyone's money management tactics be exactly the same? We do need to keep in mind that if we don't have enough on reserve, we may not be able to participate in some of those things happening now. For example, a vacation with family or night out with friends. This is just something you can keep in mind moving forward.

There have been times I've felt extremely tight on money and it made me think quite a bit about things. I've asked myself if I was going about it the right way. I mean, why was I living so tight when I had a good job? I've worked extremely hard to broaden the career opportunities I am able to pursue. These days a high school degree is not going to get you much. An associates degree will probably not get you much. A bachelors degree will get you more, but you need to also have other interpersonal skills to get your foot in the door. I knew a bachelors degree was good, but I needed more. This is why I pursued a masters degree.

Experience also will get you more opportunities in your career. As you work longer and more broadly, you are going to network more with a wider range of people. Networking will also give you more opportunities in your career. As mentioned, never write someone off just because you think they will not be beneficial to your career. First of all, that is just rude, but more importantly you never know when someone can help you down the road. It is also possible you can assist in growing their career too.

I found it very difficult earlier on in my career to get a job at a larger corporation, especially when I was at a startup company that nobody knew. In the pharmaceutical world, I applied to Johnson & Johnson, Dupont, GSK, and Merck to name a few. At this time, I spent roughly 2 years in pharmaceuticals as a chemist for my first company. I only received a few call backs for phone interviews. During this time in my life, I spent a lot of time in the laboratory setting and did not need to communicate with many people outside of my function. I was not interacting with marketing, sales, supply chain, or procurement type functions. I think this came across when I was on the phone interviews with these companies and I think this is part of the reason I did not get a call back.

If I had to do it over again, I would have tried improving my interpersonal skills. I would have became better in working in team environments. I could have been a better listener, leader, flexible, and so on. A lot of things could have been better, but this is easier said than done. When it comes to technical people, many of them do not have great interpersonal skills. This does not mean it is not a skill we should all have. Having a strong technical understanding and strong interpersonal skills can be very valuable and help you gain more opportunities.

The last piece of advice I'll mention here on career opportunities that will help you be successful is this, stay visible. Take roles that will make you visible on many fronts of the organization. This was advice I was given by a Senior Vice President of a fortune 500 company. The way I ended up receiving this advice is quite interesting and worth talking about.

During my time in packaging, I was flying from Philadelphia to Las Vegas for PackExpo. I had a connection in Dallas. Oddly enough, I was just in Las Vegas two weeks before for my friend's bachelor party, so I was not super excited about going again so quickly, especially for work. In Philadelphia while waiting for my airplane at the gate, I saw a familiar face. It was the SVP of Supply Chain for the company I worked for at the time. Although I wanted to introduce myself, I did not want to bother him. I decided I would not bother him and went back to working on my laptop at the gate.

Moments later I boarded the plane and sat in seat 12C. As I approached my seat, I looked at seat 12D and noticed the SVP was sitting there. What are the chances I am sitting next to the SVP of Supply Chain in coach, with nothing but the aisle separating us? This was too exciting for me because not many get a full two hours or so with this guy. I sat down and had my notebook on my lap. My notebook had my company's logo on the front cover. The SVP leans over and asks, if I work for that company. I told him I did and that I knew who he was, but did not want to bother him.

The SVP and myself chatted for a good portion of the two hour flight. I told him I was looking to get into supply chain and he said I could setup some time with him to talk about it. When I did eventually get back into the office I did work with his administrative assistant to setup some time. It was in that one-on-one meeting where he gave me the advice about seeking out roles that give you a lot of visibility. I did follow his recommendations and the advice was very effective. If you are good at what you do and are a hard worker, you should seek roles that give you a lot of visibility. People should know what you are doing, especially if it is good work. This will help you get promoted and move faster than if you are stuck in the basement of the company, working hard, sweating, but nobody knows what you are doing.

When opportunities are presented such as a SVP on a flight telling you to setup time with him back in the office, or someone from another team asking you to discuss an open role they have, truly think about it. Take them up on the opportunities they are presenting because most of the time the opportunities always lead you to something better. There were times when opportunities were provided, and I've said no. I played hockey with a guy who asked me to join his company as a technical sales representative. I knew this was not something I wanted and knew it would not lead to where I wanted to go. I politely declined but did stay in touch with him.

I'd also say, keep small gains in mind when you think about opportunities. An opportunity does not need to be a huge leap in career advancement from where you are today. It can be a small improvement. If that small improvement does not take you much effort to realize, then why not take advantage of the small gain? Do this several times in a year and you have just made a large gain over the course of the year. Continue pushing forward and capturing the opportunities that make sense for your career path and family. Each day, we should be working towards our goals and to do this, we need to produce results frequently.

Most of us immediately want to climb to the top right out of school and the truth is, this doesn't typically happen for most of us. At the same time, not everyone takes the same amount of time to climb the ladder in their career. Some of us simply require more time. There is no standard in terms of time required for career progression. Each one of us has different skill sets, experiences, education, and interests. Each one of us has different levels of drive and passion. Not everyone will be a high performer and that is okay. In thinking small gains, we should continually improve everyday no matter where we started from.

In thinking back to Chapter 8 – Financial Stability, I talk about the early years, middle years, and late years. The early years last 10 years, the middle years last 20 years, and the late years last 10 years. In Chapter 8, I speak in terms of salary and how we are expected to make more money later in life, especially during our late years. The last 10 years of our career is where we generate the majority of our money. These 10 years are deemed the harvest years. This makes complete sense because as we progress forward, we are expected to become more valuable with experience. Similar to this, we can also look at our career in terms of level. This can be split up between entry, intermediate, mid, and senior levels.

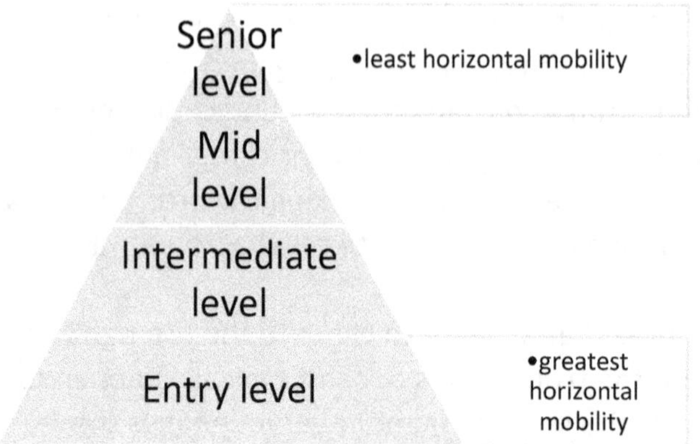

Similar to the discussion in chapter 8 focused on early, middle, and late years, we are not all going to start in the same place. The focus in chapter 8 was around salary. The focus here is on level and the understanding that we do not all start in the same place. In most cases, we may enter the workforce as entry level. There can be circumstances that you start at intermediate level or higher, especially with a graduate's degree. We can go on for days talking about different examples and where different people started, but this is not where I'd want to spend our time. It is more important to understand the pyramid from a career opportunities perspective.

In looking at the pyramid, there is a reason entry level is illustrated at the bottom in the largest base. As you are in the entry level or intermediate level range, you are more likely capable of moving around to different functions. For example, at lower levels you are not so specific that your skillset does not apply to other fields or functions across your organization. This was the reason I was able to move around from chemist to maintenance, maintenance to packaging, and packaging to supply chain. My level was not high enough where I could not move around the way I did. In the lower levels, we should take advantage of opportunities to move around to different functions for broader experiences.

The longer you are in a function or industry, the harder it will be to move around outside that function or industry. As an example, if you spent 20 years in pharmaceuticals as a chemist, you are probably going to have a difficult time finding a role at your level in another industry or function because they are not going to want to pay you what you want. If you moved to a procurement role, you are going to need to get into an entry level position, which will probably earn you less than your chemist role with 20 years of experience. This is why it is important to do much of your moving around to different functions across your company earlier on in your career. It is also possible that your company may not allow you to move around to other cross-functional groups. If this is the case, you may want to try and look outside at career opportunities with other organizations.

The point here is that you should take advantage of horizontal career progressions to different roles. It gives you a different perspective and broader experiences that others in your field may not have. When I was in R&D, I had my R&D hat on and looked at everything from an R&D lens. When I moved over to Supply Quality, I had to put my Supply Quality hat on, which was looking at those same situations from a different perspective. I quickly realized, R&D and Supply Quality had the same goal but were required to look at projects very differently. In R&D, I was pushing forward new technologies and designs to capture cost savings, improve sustainability, or improve consumer experience. In Supply Quality, I was focused on perceived risks that could cause issues, mostly from ingredient and packaging suppliers. By staying in R&D, I would have never gained the knowledge I gained when I went into Supply Quality.

I often think about the different roles across the organization and wonder what else do I not know? We can look at other workers that we work with from other teams and not fully understand what they do. We can also think they do nothing. I've heard this countless time. People will say, "those people do nothing" or "they add no value". If they stepped into those roles, would they still think those people didn't do anything? The issue is, they do not understand the value of different groups across the organization. It is purely ignorant and unacceptable on many levels. My advice is, take opportunities to work across different groups and functions. These could be some of the greatest experiences you can get and will be invaluable to your career growth. Once you spend too much time in a role or function, you may quickly find yourself pigeonholed without any other diverse opportunities. There may come a time when others view you as, *only good for one thing* and *not too versatile*.

When we think about opportunities for success and what that means, I think about a wide range of things. It goes beyond networking. It goes beyond being in the right place at the right time. Our careers should not be based on luck. We can set ourselves up for success by preparing ourselves early on in our careers. This could mean making horizontal moves to different roles across your organization to gain the experiences you need to be promoted into the positions you desire. This may also mean, moving outside your company to other organizations to gain the experiences you need that your current company does not offer. Of course, everyone has different goals and you may not require yourself to mobilize to other cross-functional groups to achieve what you set out to do. The important piece is making the most out of every day and making sure a day does not pass that you'd deem as *wasteful*. Everyday must be meaningful to you in some shape or form. Every day you should make sure you are making small gains. Taking too much on may create unbalance in our lives, which is why I approach success through small gains.

We are all capable of adjusting our lifestyles, but often we simply do not want to. It is almost an addiction of sorts where we need to repeat our lifestyle choices again and again, even if they are not appropriate. Some people choose to eat out frequently, knowing it will cost them significantly more than if they cooked a meal at home. In most cases food is less when you prepare it at home than if you were to get it from a restaurant. Plus, you do not need to leave a tip when you eat at home. If you have the money, then it's fine. If you are struggling and still eating out, then I'd have to ask why? Why are you sustaining the struggle and not making changes to improve your situation?

There will be people who take a big vacation once or twice each year. Even when times are tough, they still spend thousands on vacations because it is a big part of their lifestyle. I must ask again, why? Can they not delay the vacation for a year or two, until they can stabilize their finances? Why spend the last pennies in their account on a non-essential activity that costs more than they have? We must be discipline, especially in stringent times.

There are people out there that insist on having luxury cars, when they cannot afford luxury cars. Again, why are these people putting themselves in this situation? Purchase a vehicle that works and won't make you go bankrupt. Isn't that the logical thing to do? Although it makes sense, people do not want to sway from their lifestyle expectations. As much as I'd love to purchase a Tesla, I know it does not make sense for me right now. I can put the car in my documented goals, but purchasing it too soon, simply does not make sense and will only increase my stress.

There is a problem in our society, where people think they should have everything they want. There is no waiting until you fix your finances. There is no waiting until you have the cash to purchase the product. Everybody wants the product today and that is their expectation. Everybody has credit card debt, mortgages, student loans, auto loans, and so on. So many people are drowning in debt and because they think it is impossible to get out, they just keep driving themselves further into debt. I must ask, what the hell are they doing? This has a greater impact than they know. Our economy feels the impacts when these people go bankrupt. We all feel the pain when it is more difficult to get a mortgage because the banks have been burned so many times before.

The purpose of this chapter is to discuss the role our lifestyle plays in being successful. We can think about diets and how many people fail on diets. Plain and simple, diets don't work for the long-term because they are not normally indicative of long-term success. For starters, most people will define a starting point for the diet. I often hear people say I am going to start my diet on Monday, so they can eat whatever they please throughout the weekend. Why not just start immediately?

The diet is often something that is not sustainable throughout their lifetime. This means there is an end point, even if it's not verbalized. After this time that is spent on the diet and results are produced, you may end up going back to your old ways. Your old ways are why you were a little heavier than you would have liked to be. What makes us think going on a short diet, losing a bunch of weight, and going back to our old ways is going to make us successful long-term? To sustain your gains or losses in this example, you need to make a complete lifestyle change. This lifestyle change will last for the rest of your life, which means you need to accept the change. A diet that completely removes carbohydrates may not be sustainable for 5 or 10 years. A diet that makes you eat grapefruit every morning, may not be sustainable either.

Along the theme of small gains, we can think of gradual changes and getting those small gains frequently. If you are trying to become healthier, join a gym and start eating healthier. You need to understand that this is not just for now and it is for later too. We are to be consistent and continue to do the good things that move us forward. I could have adapted this type of thought process more in high school and in college. It was closer to the end of college when I realized quick bursts of goodness did not equate to extended wins throughout my life. I read an article about how the habits you have in college will follow you for the rest of your life. This is when I first started attending the gym regularly because I did not want to be obese.

In the first two years of college I gained twenty plus pounds of weight. Unfortunately, this was not the good type of weight such as muscle. The majority of this weight was fat. I also felt unhealthy and it lowered my self-esteem. It really hit me when I was visiting a friend at another college and he told me I was not looking healthy. This hit me like a ton of bricks. From that day, I immediately changed my lifestyle. I cut back on the unhealthy classic college foods and excessive beer. I monitored my intake and daily physical activities. The article I read about habits following you throughout your entire life also stuck out in my mind.

By the time I graduated, I was in much better shape. At the same time, I was still not satisfied with the way I looked and felt. If I stopped at graduation and did not push myself to improve my health, then I would have gone backwards and became fat once again. Constant effort to be your best is very important. Treating each decision as a lifestyle decision, is also very important. As I believe, you only get one life and should live it the best way you know how. I don't feel good about myself when I'm out of shape. Obesity has countless adverse health effects and I do not want to bring those into my life.

The financial piece is also extremely important when it comes to lifestyle choices. I briefly discussed some of the concerns I have in the start of this chapter. Making poor financial decisions or any other poor decision for that matter, only decreases our quality of life. Poor decisions lead us down a path to losing control of our life. If you do not create financial stability early on, you will have less control over what you can and cannot do. People living in poverty with very little money, have fewer choices than someone living in middle class or upper middle class. When people lose control over their life, they can start doing some pretty silly things. From a higher level, we can be judgmental about these people. I'd ask you, what would you do in their shoes?

When I visit cities and see homeless people, it is too easy to think they put themselves there. A good portion of me believes that is true, but another portion of myself believes they just had bad luck. They could have came out of a bad situation earlier on with little control over what they can and cannot do. They could also have mental illness, which is very common amongst the homeless population. I've helped out with my father down at the Atlantic City Rescue Mission where they feed the less fortunate. I've talked to quite a few homeless people and many of them are really nice. I've also noticed many of them are not the most genius of people.

Although I'd like to help all of these homeless people out who I encountered during my time helping at the Rescue Mission, it is not possible. I also know people need to help themselves out, else your help will only provide them a service for as long as you are helping. In other words, once you walk away, they are going to be back in the same place they started when you first found them. As they say, provide fish for the hungry and that will feed them for the night. Teach the hungry how to fish and that will feed them for a lifetime. This could work, but overcoming mental illnesses is a larger problem and I am not qualified to handle those types of challenges.

If there are mental illnesses present or any other type of medical issue, before you can pursue your financial goals, you are going to have to get a handle on these issues first. These may be issues you will have for the rest of your life. The point is, make sure you can manage them and not have them constantly interfering with your goals. As a professional, you want to be looked as a professional. Leave your personal problems outside of the workplace. You are not going to get promoted out of pity.

This brings me to a special point that I must make. In setting ourselves up for success, as mentioned we need to make lifestyle changes. We need to take into account our current lifestyle and understand what is not working to meet our goals. If you want to be a millionaire and are spending more money than you are making, then that is obviously a problem. If you would like to be in the best shape of your life, but are not putting in the time at the gym and eating healthy meals, then that too is a real problem. If you are looking to retire early at the age of 50 years old, but have not started saving by 40 years old, then that is obviously a problem. We need to be real with ourselves in what we can and cannot do. We need to make sure we are holding ourselves accountable for the goals we are setting.

In my younger years, when I was in high school, I did want to earn good grades. I didn't put the work in necessary to achieve those grades. Instead I would spend my time chasing girls, riding BMX bikes with friends, and doing other recreational activities similar to these. My lifestyle was built around having fun and not around success in academics. Sure, I wanted the results of good grades in school, but was not willing to put in the effort. If I did make a lifestyle change and changed the amount of time I contributed to school work, things could have been different.

Throughout my childhood, I picked up so many activities and was average at most. Perhaps I could have been above average in a few if I eliminated some of them. I was spread too thin across baseball, soccer, hockey, BMX bikes, piano, guitar, acting, and so on. If I focused on just one or two of those extra-curricular activities, could I have been much better in those areas? On the other hand, I've picked up so many skills along the way and that just means I have diverse talents.

I've spent quite a bit of time thinking about my childhood lately, especially with having children of my own. I often think about what the best way is to help them succeed. Should I put them on a more focused path where they play one sport and become the master of that sport? I think giving them a broad set of experiences will benefit them more. As discussed earlier on in this book, I talk about successful people being multi-talented. By now, most of us should already know that becoming a professional athlete is very difficult and unlikely. We also know there are many other paths in life that are both satisfying and lucrative.

We need to be real with ourselves when assessing our current situation. We need to be real with ourselves when setting goals for the future. We can say we are better off than we are and target goals that are unachievable, but who are we really trying fooling? By providing false assessments of our current situation, we are not helping ourselves achieve a successfully balanced life. In actuality, we are throwing our lives out of balance. An example can be, someone purchasing big ticket items they say they can afford, but in reality, cannot. As mentioned before, it is challenging at times to separate emotions from hard facts. Our financial trackers can help us decipher what is real and what is not. The financial tracker can assist in helping you understand how much money comes in and how much money goes out. Goals should be created from real data collected and that data can come from your financial tracker. Understanding the financial tracker data can also help you understand what you can and cannot afford.

There is a point I am trying to make here, and it is very simple. We really need to be honest with ourselves. It does not benefit us to live a lie. Although we may be passionate about living the lifestyle of the rich and famous, it is very possible we cannot afford it. It doesn't mean we will never afford it. It means we just need to start working towards it today, if you so desire that sort of lifestyle. Consistent small gains over a lengthy period of time will get you there. Holding ourselves accountable will also make sure you are not letting off the gas and will also get you there. No matter what improvement you are trying to make, you need to think in terms of long-term lifestyle changes. The shorter-term fixes can often act just like a band aid and are not always sustainable. The methods I speak of are techniques that are built for changing your lifestyle with small gains and since small gains are not intended to be overbearing, you will be able to endure, advance, and succeed more comfortably.

I've made an interesting observation on success in terms of how much pain someone can take. When we think about being successful, we may often think about the results of the work, but not always the work itself. We may also think about the rewards we will receive from being successful. I would imagine myself driving around in a fancy sports car, enjoying extravagant vacations, and living in a large house with a nice pool. Someone else's idea of success could be completely different. The important factor here is the mindset we have when it comes to success. Are we focused 100% on the end point and not the work required to get there? If so, we need to change our way of thinking.

Here is another example from high school, however we can apply this example to many areas in our lives. In high school, I can distinctively remember the students who earned above average grades. Some students could view these smarter kids as the geeks, but in reality, that was not entirely true. A lot of the smarter kids were as cool, if not cooler than the other kids who would call them geeks or nerds. Fast forward ten years, and these so-called nerds are the successful type living the good life, while the kids who were making fun of the so-called nerds, are out there breaking their back getting paid much less. So why are the smarter kids, simply smarter and more successful in school?

Several things can come into play when it comes to success in school. I would say much of these factors also apply to other areas in life, such as your career. First, these so-called nerds may have better genetics. They can simply have more brainpower than some of the other kids in their school. Of course, this is a huge advantage and should be considered. This is not the only factor that matters. The smarter kids may also like school more than some of the other kids that do not do as well. This is somewhat of a chicken or the egg first scenario. Do they like it more because they've been good at school or were they good in school, so that is why they like it?

Another factor in why kids may do well in school is their support system. Their family will be their biggest support system in most cases at this age. Friends and teachers will also be part of their support system. Good teachers will be able to help further their students' growth and learning. Friends are extremely important because we are usually like our friends. If our friends deem education as important, then most likely we are going to also deem education as important. If our friends are drug addicts, we are most likely going to be drug addicts or at least tried drugs. Why else would we be hanging out with that group? Common interests bring us together. These correlations are backed by statistics. We need to choose our friends wisely.

Here is a factor that I never really thought about until recent years. Tolerance of struggle, pain, uncomfortable situations, or seemingly endless required effort is a factor in whether you are going to be successful or not. It sounds a bit weird, but I assure you it makes complete sense. When we set out to reach a goal, as mentioned we might focus more on the rewards we will see from reaching that goal. We need to make sure we are building a reasonable plan to achieve the goal in a timely manner. This goal is to be documented and reviewed as frequently as you deem necessary. We must also set expectation, that work is required and that we might fail several times before achieving the goal.

We can also think about tolerance when we think about working out at the gym. When we workout, we are stressing our bodies, and this can be uncomfortable. This is a big reason so many do not commit to a lifestyle of working out continuously. Similarly, diets can also be uncomfortable, which is why so many only go on diets for a short period of time. In school, students who cannot tolerate the schoolwork, will simply not succeed. We can also talk about it in terms of a job, where those who cannot tolerate their job, will not be a high performer. Perseverance is an important quality to have if you do want to succeed. There is no getting around it. Those who cannot persevere will throw in the towel too quickly and not succeed.

I will note perseverance and tolerance are interchangeable words. When we persevere, we continue down a course of action or path without regard to discouragement or opposition or failure. Tolerance is the ability to endure pain or hardship. In my eyes, these are roughly the same meaning. Although, when we think of the two words it feels as if perseverance has a more positive brand than tolerance. Most people would rather say, I tolerate my annoying sister. Very few would say, I persevere when it comes to my sister. So, why do I bring up this point? Quite simply, to make note of the fact that there are words we can use for certain situations that fit or sound right, and other words don't. Either way, perseverance and tolerance are pretty much the same thing. Before, I go off the beaten path too much, let's get back to the subject at hand.

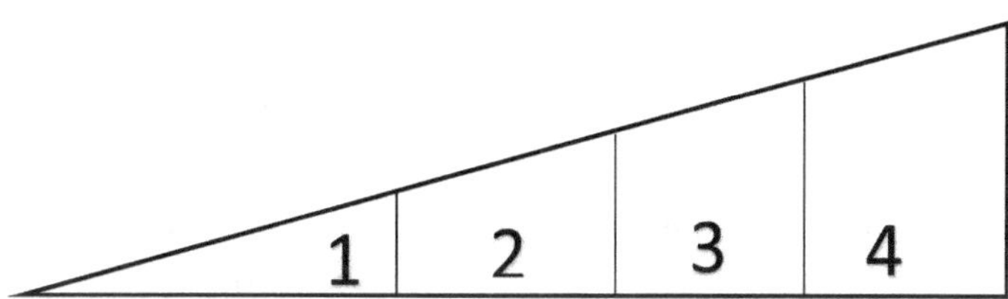

Here we have an illustration of a tolerance rating system from 1 thru 4, where 1 is lowest tolerance and 4 is highest tolerance. We may be extremely tolerant people at level 4, when it comes to family matters, but extremely intolerant people at level 1, when it comes to politics. We can be extremely tolerant people at level 4, when it comes to dealing with lazy people, but extremely intolerant people at level 1, when it comes to dealing with liars. Everybody has difference in what they are able to tolerate and not tolerate, which is where this tolerance rating system comes into play.

Now, let's think about this same 1 thru 4 system, as now being a perseverance rating system. You may be able to persevere through intensive studying at level 4, but not able to endure much physical fitness at level 1. You may be able to endure tons of pushback whenever you try to advance in your career. You may be able to endure the struggle of not finding a romantic partner, or maybe the opposite is true where you cannot endure this hardship. When I think perseverance, I typically think of the endurance required to be successful and produce results. When I think tolerance, I think about the annoyances along the way. Although, both perseverance and tolerance are roughly the same thing, the branding and messaging are slightly different.

Here is what I am getting at. We need to understand how much we can endure when we set our goals and strategy to get there. If we take on too much, too soon, it will be a disaster and we will not reach our goals. The truth is, too many cannot persevere and give up too soon, before reaching their goals. I speak from personal experience and this can be unsettling, when we start digging into the truth. Why are we so easy to break at times, when in other times, we are so solid and unbreakable? Why can we tolerate some things, while not tolerating others? Why can we show so much perseverance at times, while having no endurance or perseverance at other times?

This all goes back to our personal experiences and what makes us tick. I am a very patient man 99% of the time, but there is that 1% of the time that I cannot take it. When it comes to enduring pain through working out at the gym, or realizing I've failed to achieve a goal, I will continue pushing forward. Then there's that small thing somebody does, that annoys me to no end, and it typically is because of the specific person doing it. A lot of times, I am most annoyed by people I've known the longest, and I cannot explain why. At the end of the day, these small annoyances cannot blur your vision on what is really important. Too often, we get upset over the small things and need to realize, there's a much bigger picture out there. The world is going to keep spinning and this small bothersome issue, will not come in the way of that. So, why let this small issue get in the way of our big dreams?

The next time, you are bothered by something, think about what and why it is bothering you? Take some time, to really think about what that thing is. Take some time, to think about who the people are involved. Try to remember your goals and how you cannot lose focus on those goals, because they are more important. I can give an example happening now in many of our lives. There is a presidential election coming up in 2020 between President Donald Trump and former Vice President Joe Biden. People on both sides are troubled and worried if the other candidate wins. I've had struggles of my own with this topic because I too am very worried if my candidate does not win. But why am I becoming overly upset about this? So, what if the other guy wins? Does it really impact me? I guess it could, but I can always prepare for what I'd think is the worst.

Another example might be a neighbor you don't get along with, and you let it consume your life. Anytime you see them outside, it annoys you and you are more focused on them instead of your own household. I've also seen people get too wrapped up in social media such as Facebook or Instagram. People are more curious about someone else's life instead of their own life. We all have interesting things going on in our lives, but we can get too deep into digging into other people's lives. Why does this happen?

In 2009, I found myself getting too caught up in other people's lives on Facebook. I would not say I was more excessive than anyone else, but I quickly realized it was unhealthy for my personal goals. The time I spent on Facebook could have been used to drive forward things that actually mattered. In 2009, I ended my Facebook account because it was the right thing to do. I have consistently limited myself from spending too much time on social media because, it doesn't help me reach my goals. I replaced social media with efforts to push forward my agenda such as learning useful information, improving my skills in various areas, and executing tasks to push forward my career, business, and personal life. So, what does this have to do with perseverance?

In life, we are faced with decisions every day and people who want to influence us to do stuff, that might be more beneficial to them, then ourselves. For instance, Facebook would generate money from me being on there, surfing around, and giving them personal information or data. I am not necessarily paying for the service directly by providing them cash, but I am giving them time, which is extremely valuable. Similarly, Instagram or any other social media service is collecting your information and offering you services or products through advertisements. Those companies advertising are paying Facebook or Instagram top dollar, because Facebook and Instagram know your interests from your search histories and what you've liked in the past. They know much more about you than you are aware.

Additionally, I've had friends ask me why I am not on Facebook. There is something powerful about everyone else participating in something, which tends to influence you to do the same. Although I do have Instagram, I often wonder if I should. I still have stayed off Facebook since 2009 because I do not want to participate and that is my choice.

There are choices in our lives that we will need to make, and those choices may be difficult. We may have people trying to influence us to do something else, that may benefit them more than ourselves. In my earlier years, I was more readily influenced by my peer group and this can be an issue at times. My younger self was less likely to think anything bad could happen to me. I felt as if I were invincible, but we all know this was not true. I have failed too many times to remember. The important part is, I did learn from my mistakes and kept going. I did persevere, but too many do not. So, I can ask myself why I was able to persevere, while others do not? And a large part of this, is my support system and my drive to be successful.

There was a time in college when I did get in trouble with the law. This was a very dark time in my life. As a college student, I was doing what everyone else was doing with my roommates. We were throwing parties every weekend and getting pretty good at it. At some point, the local authorities felt it was too much and decided to shut us down. Myself and four out of my five roommates did get in trouble. The one roommate who did not get in trouble was there but did a very nice job of hiding. After it was all said and done, I admit we were wrong and should have never been throwing the parties for so many reasons. At this point, I did feel pretty down and wanted to quit on myself. I was willing to stop going to school and move away. I probably would have, if it weren't for my father.

I know my mother and father knew I needed support and reassurance, so my father would frequently drive 90-minutes up to visit me. He would take me out to eat and talk to me. He was not willing to give up on me and told me to remain patient. Basically, the same advice he has always given me my entire life, and this meant the world to me. During these darker times of my life, we became much closer and I was able to learn a lot about him and his family. I always wondered why my father was so patient with my brother and me. How could he put up with some of the dumb stuff we did? I finally realized, everything we did was insignificantly small in relation to some of the bad stuff he has seen in his life. He had seen a lot worse and went through a lot worse. He has persevered and tolerated so much worse than I ever had.

There were times in my father's life when they did not have a house because it burned down. There were times in my father's life when he could not play on a baseball team because they were too poor. My entire life, he was always giving so much to everyone else in our family, but never bought himself anything. He always said, "as long as everyone else is happy, then I'm happy". I never really understood this until I had my own children, and it really is true. Your children's' happiness is everything. We can persevere through almost anything, if we have purpose. And that is a very big key takeaway here. We need purpose or we are driving to nowhere.

It all comes back to knowing where we are going and why we are going there. It all comes back to making sure we are documenting our goals and building a strong strategic plan to get there. Whenever I think about my goals and why I want them so badly, I always think about my parents and everything they've done for my brother and me. Without their unrelentless perseverance in their younger years, to rise above all challenges, they'd never be where they are today, and I'd not be where I am.

If we try to take it all on, all at one time, it becomes too cumbersome and we'd probably fail. It becomes too discouraging to try and climb an entire mountain in one day. We need to take it piece by piece, to make the trek more bearable. It is up to us, to rate our tolerance or perseverance, as shown earlier on in this chapter from 1 thru 4. If this scaling system doesn't work, then you can create your own, as long as it works for you. When you map out your goals and each step of the way, you must understand how much you can do each day, each week, each month, or each year. You must know what is reasonable because unrealistic goals are probably going to discourage you.

As an example, I wanted to pay off my mortgage as fast as I possibly could. I could have dumped everything I earned into my mortgage, but knew I'd not be able to really do much else. This was not a sustainable plan for the long term. I determined 8-10 years was a reasonable amount of time to pay off my mortgage. I then put into my written plan that I'd pay roughly 10% to 12.5% of my mortgage each year on average. Obviously, there is a curve in paying off debt because you are paying highest interest in the beginning and lowest interest towards the end. The point here is, I setup a plan that was reasonable and that would not be discouraging. I knew this was something I could endure throughout the course of the 8 to 10 years of paying my mortgage. This is how we should be thinking about these things.

At the end of the day, perseverance is extremely important to our success story. We must understand our purpose behind why we are doing what we are doing and be able to work through the struggles that are both expected and unexpected. Our support system, including our family, friends, mentors, and other support counterparts can really help us through some of our most challenging times. As mentioned, we can use a rating system on how much we can tolerate or persevere, or we can simply just say, "I can" or "I cannot tolerate". If we are able to know ourselves and why we do the things we do, we can really use this to our advantage. As a thinking species, we should be able to control our emotions, and really think about our next actions. Getting too excited is rarely a good thing. We must persevere to achieve our success story and I don't think there is any way around it.

My grandpa is 93 years old and has lived a remarkable life, or at least I think so. There have been some troubling times in his life, but he has always focused on the positive and I am starting to realize why. It seems super obvious, but to many people, it is more comfortable to live in fear and negativity. Many people are somehow comforted by the gloominess of this world, more so than the cheery upbeat joys of this world. We can both be pragmatic and optimistic. I do not see how the two need to cancel each other out. In actuality, being pragmatic better sets us up for future success and happiness.

Throughout my grandpa's life who we call 'Papi', he has worked to make this world a better place. No matter if it were through his career in his younger years or working as a member for his local tennis club or working as president or treasurer for the Lion's Club, he has brought his leadership skills and positive attitude. He has special skills in gardening, and it seems to have brought him peace. Much of what he does today is very consistent with what he has done in his younger years, and I see this consistency trait in myself. For example, I have consistently written in my journal nearly every day since June 15th of 2005. Over 15 years later, I am still writing in this longstanding journal because it works for me. I have no doubt the trait of being consistent was passed down from my grandpa to me.

I also know my grandpa had to make many difficult decisions in his life. Since he is a leader and has good moral fiber, he has typically always made the right decisions. For one, he did not join the communist party in

Chile, when it could have made things much easier for him and his family. He knew it was wrong, and there was suffering going on because of it. He knew this was not the right thing to do, so he held out. I would hope I would make the same decision if it came down to it. I would hope I could be brave enough to truly stick to my beliefs, but you never really know until you are put in that situation. It's much easier to talk about what we'd do, when we are not yet faced with the circumstance in our lives.

My grandpa who is no longer alive today, which is my father's father, was also said to be strong and a great man. Although he did not make too much money driving trucks, he consistently worked and worked hard. This hardworking gene was passed down to my father and eventually, this gene was passed down to me. It doesn't matter what you are doing, as long as you are doing it and proud of what you are doing. I'm not really sure if my grandpa Jerry was big into driving trucks, but I do know he never gave up. These are the values and characteristics that I want my children to have. Not everyone is going to be a CEO, doctor, lawyer, or entrepreneur. The important thing is, we have a plan and know where we are going.

When I say, *Balancing Life with Small Gains*, I am talking about managing your life fairly with respect. Since it is your life, then you are responsible for setting the rules and guidelines that you must follow. If you want to spend lots of time with your family and never miss your son's baseball game, then you must respect those wishes. If you are working too much and are missing your son's baseball game, then you are simply disrespecting your wishes. There are times we need to sacrifice but do need to understand the implications of those sacrifices. We need to set boundaries and make sure we are not crossing those boundaries too frequently. Maybe you allow yourself to miss one game, but never miss another for the remaining season. If you start creating excuses for missing more, you are starting to lose your grounding and will start suffering because of it. Don't lose sight of your core values.

During the earlier years when I first had my son Benjamin, I did need to travel a bit more. I was flying out quite a bit and did not enjoy being away. To solve for this, I started to really prioritize my travel and push back when it was not necessary. For starters, I just don't like jumping on airplanes for the hell of it. Not being home to see my son growing up is somewhat dark. Knowing that I only get one chance to see him hit key milestones like first words and first steps, I knew I needed to adjust. I also knew whenever my second child came along, I wanted to also be around for him too. This is when I realized that I could switch career paths once again and travel a bit less. I ended up going back into Packaging Engineering with the promise of less traveling.

In my career, each step of the way I have climbed a considerable amount when you look at start to now. If I break it up and see what changes happened from day to day, week to week, and month to month, the changes are actually quite small. My knowledge slowly built up overtime, as I worked on various projects through my career. My network grew slowly, but steadily since I first started working. The first couple years as a chemist, my network did not grow too quickly because I spent most of my time in a laboratory with very few people. My salary also grew slowly towards the earlier part of my career.

Looking back at myself as a high school student, I can now realize the lack of passion I truly had. I did not have a focused plan because I did not know where I wanted to go. I did not feel confident about myself, which is pretty normal for high school students. I could have done better in school and ended up getting into a 4-year university sooner. As mentioned, when I did end up going away to university, I ended up having to really push myself. For all the years earlier on in high school I slacked off, I was really paying for it in college. I finally found that I needed prove my commitment to succeeding. As mentioned in Chapter 2, commitment is a very big piece to succeeding. Without commitment, we are going to have a very challenging time driving our efforts forward to hit our goals.

I have also spoke about learning from others and how crucial it is, because it can save ourselves time. We don't necessarily have to overdose on drugs to know it isn't the smartest thing to do. We don't have to get in a bad car accident while being drunk, to know it isn't the smartest thing to do. As important as it is to learn from others' successes, it is equally important to learn from others' failures. Not all knowledge we gain will come to us overnight. We must be interested in learning and consistently drive ourselves to learn. Over a longer period of time, we can gain a considerable amount of knowledge by simply learning bits and pieces of information along the way.

I have also spoke about setting and tracking your goals because this is crucial to holding yourself accountable. If you do not remember what your goal is, then how would you know if you hit it? I could say, I want to own a successful business, which is pretty vague. First of all, when should this be done and what key performance indicators are set in place to track it? Additionally, if I don't document this goal anywhere, how long will go by before I forget about this goal? If it were that meaningful to you, then you may just always remember. However, most of us have multiple goals that we'd like to hit. I may want a family, build a successful career, become a volunteer firefighter, and run a half-marathon. Over the course of a year or two years, how would I remember all of this? How could I remember to track and evaluate my progress? For me, I simply need to document all of these activities, so I can monitor my progress.

In chapter 5, I spoke about small gains and what smalls gains really are. A small gain is any advancement relatively small in size, which is layered with more small gains at later dates or times, to build something much larger. The strategy is built around not overly exhausting yourself, or working too hard on a specific task, where you'd want to throw in the towel too early. I am not saying you should not push hard for your goals, but it is also possible to chew small amounts at a time and achieve the same goal, as if you were to chew the whole meal all at once. There is a famous saying, don't bite off more than you can chew. I feel this holds very true and it's really timeless.

It truly is the small gains that can help us keep our lives balanced while obtaining our goals. As mentioned earlier on, we do only have 24 hours in a day. There's no way to add time to the day, but we can become more efficient in what we do, to make the most of it. We can also prioritize what we do, to make the greatest impacts. There was a time I would read all my emails at the start of any day on the job. By the time I was done reading and responding, I had very little time to accomplish my own objectives because I was too busy helping others out. Where is the balance in this? How do I advance my own career when I am too busy helping other's advance theirs? Stephen Covey has some interesting philosophies on time management that I have studied, and I'd recommend you look into these, especially his bit on big rocks.

There are a few authors like Stephen Covey and Dale Carnegie that I have read and studied. These are guys who have helped me learn and optimize my life. I did not read every book they had overnight. I did it piece by piece, as I knew it would take time. Following my small gains philosophies, I was able to learn a great amount over several years. As much as we want to learn everything today and be successful today, that is not the way it works. We need to make sure we have a goal in mind or destination where we want to be. We then layout a path to get there and try including all the potential challenges in between. Our plan would account for possible failures. We are responsible for being able to endure these failures through perseverance and toleration, as talked about in Chapter 12.

Our support systems, including family, friends, co-workers, mentors, managers, and so on will help us through our rough patches. As mentioned in Chapter 6, family is important and a crucial part to our success story. For most of us, we are doing the hard work to provide greater opportunities for our children, grandchildren, and great grandchildren. We are making the tough decisions like both my grandpas, to make sure our youth have a brighter future. I'd not feel good about myself if I had to tell my children they couldn't play baseball because we were short on funds. At some point, my father was told this because they did not have the funds for him to play. I am sure that was not an easy conversation. I am sure there are more kids out there than we know, with similar stories. I cannot help everyone but can certainly help my kids and that is what I plan on doing.

At the top of all my pillars there's an idea larger than anything else, which I do not often talk about. It's simplistic and real. It is the idea of happiness! In Chapter 4 titled, *Setting and tracking your goals*, I show the *Pillars to success*, as illustrated here.

Pillars to success

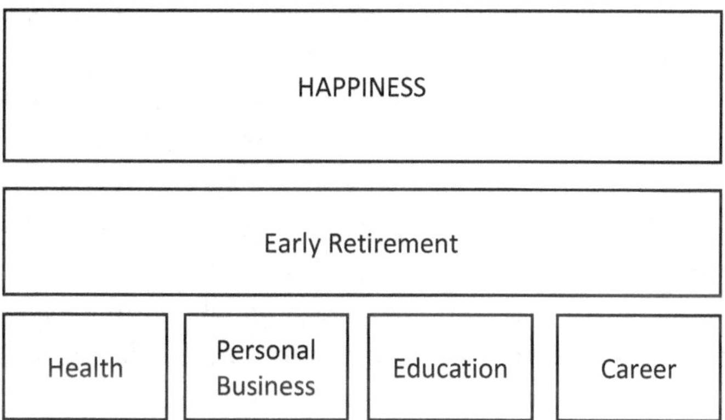

The difference in Chapter 4 is I do not have the top box with the text inside – *HAPPINESS*. Everybody should really have this box above their goals because it truly is what we all want, or at least that's what I'd think everyone would want. The importance of mentioning this is to say, we can achieve our goals without ending up happy. How can this be possible? For my example, I want to retire or at least have the option of early retirement. I have laid out 4 pillars – health, personal business, education, and career. It is very possible I can get to early retirement and still not be happy. This would probably happen if I ended up getting to early retirement in poor health. If I achieved early retirement through unethical means, then I'd also not be too happy with myself. If I achieved early retirement by working too hard and missing out on spending much time with my family, then I'd also not be happy. There needs to be a balance in our lives to achieve happiness.

There are real guardrails that need to be in place when we are trying to achieve our goals. These guardrails are set in place, so we can achieve what we want in a healthy manner, without giving up our core values. There's always the story about the guy who got everything he wanted by selling his soul to the devil. If you needed to sell your soul to the devil, then you are probably better off never reaching your goals. It is never good doing business with the devil. For instance, if you want to be a millionaire and you start selling drugs to get there, you are doing more harm than good. If you rob a bank to get the money, you are doing more harm than good. If you are participating in anything that isn't moral, you are doing more harm than good.

We really need to balance our lives with small gains, and in rare occasions take the leap for a larger gain. Always be consistent and intentional. Be confident to push yourself forward and drive the results you are looking for but make certain you are doing it with good ethic. Poor behaviors lead to poor outcomes, and this I have experienced firsthand. Whatever your defined pillars are to reach your overarching goals, you need to be accepting of the path you take to get there. An unpleasant path can lead to unwelcoming results. We must also ask ourselves, if we are okay with others knowing what we've done to get where we want to go? In other words, are we proud of what we've done and who we've become? If both of these can be answered 'yes', then we are most probably on the right path.

The intent of this book is not to drill down and make anyone feel bad. The intent of this book is to shed light on some subjects that are fascinating to me, and hopefully you. I have spent many years gathering information and trying to make sense of it. Money management type topics are sometimes not common in households, but why not? I think teaching our children this subject is crucial to their future success in their lives. You do not need to make millions every year to be a millionaire. You can simply save up these smaller gains over a longer period of time, and it would still result in you being a millionaire. Paying down debts, investing, and building your retirement fund are critical steps to building financial stability. I am hopeful this book can and will shed light on these topics, and the strategies I've used.

For me, a wealthier, more prosperous world is better for everyone. More money generated means more taxes paid amongst the broader population, meaning theoretically, we should each only need to pay our share. By this I mean, everyone is capable of providing for themselves and fewer handouts are needed. As a population, we become smarter and more capable of handling our own families. Everyone should be entitled to a quality life with no fear of financial burden. I have seen some poor living conditions, especially around my town when the blueberry pickers come into town and stay at local rural farm camps. Those camps are no Holiday Inn. I put myself in the shoes of those pickers from Haiti and Mexico. I think about my own children living there and it deeply saddens me. How can we help these people out? Should we help these hard-working people out?

 When I think about balancing life with small gains, I do think about these blueberry pickers, who I have had many conversations with. My father and I work out of a shop in the middle of a blueberry field, and these pickers walk by. Often, they will stop and talk to us. They ask us what we are building and are very cordial. At the end of the day, my father and I go back to our homes that are comfortable and well air conditioned. The pickers go back to their camps, where they sleep on uncomfortable bunk beds and all the walls are cinder block and not very pretty to look at. My father and I have bought them groceries on countless occasions. We have given them a few dollars, but it's never enough. How do they get ahead? How do they advance?

They may never advance in this lifetime. They may need several lifetimes to advance into a better quality of living. What is important is that they work on the small gains and persevere. I truly believe they can build a better life for themselves, just like my parents did. It is possible they can work and save enough money to build themselves a better life. But, if they were to give up today because they felt overwhelmed by it all, that would never happen. The truth is, in America we are blessed with opportunity, no matter who you are. It may be true, we all start at different starting locations. It may be true, we are looked at a little differently based on what we look like or how we sound. But the truth is, we can all succeed and it has been proven time and time again.

We can think about the blueberry pickers across America. We can think about the less fortunate living arrangements in third world countries across the globe. And now, think about our own living situation and where you started. There are programs out there to help the misfortunate. There are support systems out there if you are willing to look. We can truly balance life with small gains, but we really do need to start today. Waiting for tomorrow can be tragic when tomorrow never comes. If you don't give yourself a chance, then why would anyone else? No matter where you are starting from, you deserve a better life.

This is your chance to really go out there and show the world what you are made of. You can start your path to success today, by making small gains each day. Document your failures and accomplishments, so you can remember them at a later date to reflect. We are all capable of reaching success, no matter who we are. I believe we only live once, so it is our obligation to make things happen in this lifetime, because you are not going to get another opportunity. The opportunity is now, and we must all take this opportunity to succeed. We can live balanced and achieve greatness. We don't need to exhaust ourselves and can really drive results in a controlled manner. The opportunity to win starts now.